Equality, Diversity, & Inclusion:

The practical guide

2021

Second Edition

First Published 2009 limited private run.

First edition, 2018

This second edition, 2021

ISBN: 9798595510806

02-01-01

Published by
Mendip Hills Studio Ltd

Thank you to colleagues and friends old and new from all communities who help review, check, edit, and advise on this project.

This title is dedicated to Gaby Charring, a lifelong campaigner who showed us above all dignity for each other is the foundation of Human Rights.

Published and printed using an environmentally considered process.

tonymalone.co.uk

Equality, Diversity, & Inclusion:

The practical guide

Dr Tony Malone

Second Edition

2021

Contents

Preface to the Second Edition

December 2021

Wow Thank you! When I tentatively put the first edition of this Book together, I did not anticipate it taking off in such a way. Fast becoming one of the most read books for Equality, Diversity and Inclusion around the world. Thank you for buying it, reading it, sharing and creating a better world with it!

I have had some wonderful letters, comments and suggestions, many of which have helped collectively shape this new 2021 Edition. As we move into a "new world" post the COVID-19 Pandemic let's remember it is an opportunity to re-shape our society into something more compassionate and more inclusive. Let us create a better world where no one is left out or behind.

Tony.

Introduction

In many years of providing talks on Human Rights, Inclusion and I find I am frequently asked the same questions...

"What's the right word for...", "How do I say...", "Am I racist if I use this term...".

All these questions are based in two principles, first how to communicate effectively, and secondly a genuine commitment to being kind to one another.

I've produced, reviewed and updated many handouts over the years, many of which I find are still just as useful now as they were twenty years ago. Others, updates to language and terminology are needed.

Language evolves, society moves forwards in complexity and in recognition of communities and human rights. This is the future being written by our past being challenged and scrutinised in the present.

I've developed this handbook not as a one stop source book, but as a springboard. One which I hope gives the user, -not the reader-, a quick reference point to assist with terms, language or interfaith and cultural dialogue.

I make a point of the word user over reader as I fully anticipate that no one would read this book, but they will hopefully use it as they would any other tool for equality and inclusion.

At the end of this guide there is a means to contact myself for anything you disagree with, would like to change, or suggest for future editions. I am very happy for pages of this title to be photocopied, shared and passed around if it is useful, just please reference where it came from.

Lastly, remember your own interest in Equality, Diversity, Rights and all it entails has come from wanting to make the world a better more inclusive place.

Please never stop changing the world for the better!

We shall Overcome, Today.

Painted by Tony in 2020.

How to use this guide

Aims of this guide

Firstly, don't read this cover to cover, unless you really want to! It is intended as a guide and reference book.

I would suggest the best way to use this guide is simply when you need a term, want to learn about a new faith or community, look them up in the terminology or guides. Use the contents page at the start to shape your use of this book, the same way you would a Thesaurus or encyclopaedia perhaps.

The overall aims of this guide are to help people communicate more effectively and respectfully with one another.

Bias within this guide

As with all areas of Equality, Diversity and Inclusion it is important to acknowledge and overcome any bias, unconscious bias and privilege inherent in its creation. To that end, I should point out there is a UK and Westernised Bias within this book due to its author, editors, and contributors combined location and outlook. However we hope we have overcome this where possible and any other form of bias within this title. If you would like to discuss this with us, there is a section at the back about how to contact us to suggest alterations for future editions. An Arabic and Korean language edition of this title is being prepared.

The Glossary

Using the glossary

This glossary is not intended to be an exhaustive list of every word and term used in our many conversations about diversity, inclusion, and social justice. These are basic working definitions to be used as a reference to help move your diversity and inclusion efforts forward.

Ability

Power or capacity to do or act physically, mentally, legally, morally, financially, etc.

Ableism

Dominant attitudes in society that assume there is an ideal body and mind, leading to discriminatory behaviours toward people who differ from this society imposed 'normality'.

Access

The necessary conditions so that individuals and organisations desiring to, and who are eligible to, use services, facilities, information, programmes and employment opportunities in an equal way.

Accessibility

Creating the necessary conditions so that individuals and organisations can access goods, services, programmes, etc in an equal and dignified way.

Affinity bias

The tendency to connect with people who look and seem most like ourselves.

Affinity groups

A group of people who share the same interest or purpose such as gender, age, religion, race or sexual orientation.

Affirmative action

The practice / policy of favouring individuals belonging to groups known to have been discriminated against previously.

Age

The biological age of a person's body since their birth.

Age (Mental or cognitive)

The medically assumed age of a person's mind due to learning difficulties or injury. This is not something that should ever be assumed or pre-judged.

Age discrimination

Often not taken as seriously as other forms of discrimination. However, it can have the same economic, social and psychological impact as any other form of discrimination. This affected people of all ages.

Ageism

The term "ageism" refers to two concepts:

- a socially constructed way of thinking about older or younger persons based on negative attitudes and stereotypes about their age.

- a tendency to structure society based on an assumption that everyone is young, thereby failing to respond appropriately to the real needs of older persons.

Agender

Those whose gender identity does not align with any gender.

Ally

A person of one social identity group who stands up in support or in alliance of members of another group; typically, member of dominant identity advocating and supporting a marginalised group.

Androgynous

A person who does not identify or present as solely feminine nor masculine.

Anti-Oppression

Strategies, theories and actions that challenge social and historical inequalities and injustices that are systemic to our systems and institutions by policies and practices that allow certain groups to dominate over other groups.

Anti-Racism

An active and consistent process of change to eliminate individual, institutional and systemic racism.

Anti-Racist Education

A perspective that promotes the identification and change required of educational practices, policies, attitudes and behaviours that underlie racism.

Antisemitism

Latent or overt hostility or hatred directed towards, or discrimination against individual Jews or the Jewish people for reasons connected to their religion, ethnicity, and their cultural, historical, intellectual and religious heritage. Antisemitism has also been expressed through individual acts of physical violence, vandalism, the organized destruction of entire communities and genocide. In more recent times, such manifestations could also target the state of Israel, conceived as a Jewish collective.

Asexual

A person who is not sexually attracted to anyone or does not have a sexual orientation. They may or may not experience romantic attraction.

Asian

Specific term for people of East Asian origin. It is better to be more specific and respectful if possible, in its usage. i.e. East Asian, South Asian, Indian, Chinese, Korean, etc.

Atheism

Disbelief or lack of belief in the existence of God or gods.

Attribution error

Using a false assumption to explain someone's behaviour based on their diversity or characteristics.

B

Barrier

A physical or societal structure, design, practice or rule that prevents or impedes individuals from accessing a service or community life.

Background

The community, education, race, ethnicity, and or employment of a person.

Behavioural diversity

Behavioural Diversity relates to personal experiences that help shape our world view to be more open-minded and accepting of others who are different than us.

Bi

An attraction towards more than one gender. Bi people may also describe themselves as bisexual, pansexual, bi-curious, queer, and other non-monosexual identities.

Bi-cultural

Bicultural identity is the condition of being oneself regarding the combination of two cultures.

Bias

A subjective opinion, preference, prejudice or inclination, often formed without reasonable justification that influences an individual's or group's ability to evaluate a situation objectively or accurately, a preference for or against. Reasonable apprehension of bias exists when there is a reasonable belief that an individual or group will pre-judge a matter and therefore cannot assess a matter impartially because of bias.

Biphobia

The fear or hatred of bisexual individuals.

Bigender

A term associated with someone identifying as both man and woman.

Bisexuality

A sexual orientation in which a person has the potential to feel physically and emotionally attracted to more than one gender or sex.

Blind

Blind or partially sighted person, person with little or no sight, visual impairment.

Black

'Black people' generally refers either to people of African or Afro-Caribbean origin, including African-American or people born elsewhere with African or Afro- Caribbean heritage.

BME (sometimes: BAME)

Black, Minority, Ethnic. A 'blanket' term used frequently for people of non-European white origin. It should only be used when appropriate with this context. Therefore, it is best to avoid generalisations of experience: it is better to state what groups are being discussed in a particular context.

Butch

Refers to a person with an overtly/stereotypically masculine or masculine-acting woman. Often used to denote the dominant role in a lesbian relationship.

Cisgender or Cis

A term denoting a person whose gender identity aligns with their assigned sex.

Closeted

Someone who is not disclosing their true sexual orientation or gender identity.

Classism

The cultural, institutional and individual set of practices and beliefs that assign value to people according to their socio-economic status, thereby resulting in differential treatment.

Cognitive diversity

Cognitive diversity accounts for differences in our perspective and the way we process information.

Cognitive Impairment

A Disabled Person with intellectual, emotional or learning difficulty.

Coming Out

The process through which a person acknowledges and accepts their sexual orientation or gender identity and shares this with others.

Confirmation bias

Seeking out or only noticing information that reinforces our existing beliefs.

Conscious prejudice

Preconceived, usually negative, feelings towards people based solely on their group membership, like religion, race, ethnicity or age.

Cover

An action where an individual intentionally downplays or omits disclosure of known stigmatized identity to fit in with the dominant culture.

Creative abrasion

A culture and a practice where ideas are productively challenged. It's about having heated, yet healthy, arguments to generate a portfolio of alternative ideas.

Culture

A way of life of a group of people--the behaviours, beliefs, values, and symbols that they accept, generally without thinking about them, and that are passed along by communication and imitation from one generation to the next.

Cultural Competence

This refers to an ability to interact effectively with people of different cultures.

Cultural competence comprises four components:

- Awareness of one's own cultural worldview

- Attitude towards cultural differences

- Knowledge of different cultural practices and worldviews.

- Cross-cultural skills.

Developing cultural competence results in an ability to understand, communicate with, and effectively interact with people across cultures. Cultural competence is a developmental process that evolves over an extended period.

Culture fit

Individual attitudes, values, behaviours, and beliefs being in line with the core values and culture of an organization.

Cultural Literacy

Also known as Cultural Humility or Intercultural Competence it is the acquisition of awareness, knowledge and skills required to communicate, work and live effectively in a pluralistic society.

Cross-dresser

A person wearing clothing stereotypically worn by the other sex but has no intention to live full-time as the other sex.

Deadnaming

Calling someone by their birth name after they have changed their name. Often associated with trans people who have changed their name.

Deaf

A person with an audible impairment. It is suggested to use the term 'Hearing Impairment instead of 'Deaf' as a less familiar term. It should be noted that the Deaf community is a sub-culture with its own language, history and traditions and is not always seen as a disability, simply, different. It is always good practice to never make assumptions, criticisms and be open and honest if asking questions to gain insight or knowledge.

Development (SDGs)

The progress of a person, entity or organisation towards meeting and supporting the UN Sustainable Development Goals (SDGs)

D&I

An acronym that stands for diversity and inclusion. Often in organisations which avoid or separate Equality terms in their work or management. Preferred term is 'EDI" to include Equality.

Dignity

A fundamental Human Right protected by the UN Universal Declaration of Human Rights. To ensure that everyone is treated equally and respectfully at all times.

Disability

A physical, mental or cognitive impairment or condition that requires adjustments are made to society, workplace, project, programme etc., to ensure fair and equal access in a dignified way. It is important to note that a medically imposed label is a stigma and serves to undermine Disabled People's rights and so therefore should be avoided.

Disabled People

The community accepted term to describe the community of people whom are disabled by the environment or society.

Discrimination

Discrimination - Denial of fair and equitable treatment, civil liberties and or opportunity. The subornation of people or groups resulting in unequal treatment and deprivation of political, social and economic rights. It is often invisible to those who are not its targets, or those who enjoy power and privilege in a society. Discrimination can be individual or systemic and may be absent of intent. Can be created by a bias or favouritisms.

Discrimination (active)

Deliberately creating circumstances or deliberate acts to discriminate. I.e. Racism, Sexism, Homophobia.

Discrimination (passive)

Institutional bias or complex/late adjustments to create accessibility. Ignorance or in action creating circumstances where discrimination can develop without direct influence.

Diaspora

A scattered population which originated from a different geographical area.

Diversity

Psychological, physical, and social differences that occur among any and all individuals; including but not limited to race, colour, ethnicity, nationality, religion, socioeconomic status, veteran status, education, marital status, language, sex, age, gender, gender expression, gender identity, sexual orientation, mental or physical ability, genetic information and learning styles. A diverse group, community, or organization is one in which a variety of social and cultural characteristics exist.

Dominant Culture

A cultural practice that is dominant within a particular political, social or economic entity, in which multiple cultures are present. It may refer to a language, religion/ritual, social value and/or social custom.

Dominant Group

Not necessarily a majority in terms of numbers, but the group with power, privilege and social status in a society. Attributes of this group are accepted as the 'norm' by which other groups are measured or compared, often to their detriment.

Drag King

Female performers who dress as men for entertainment at clubs and events.

Drag Queen

Male performers who dress as women for entertainment at clubs and events.

E

Economically disadvantaged

A person living at or below poverty line, people experiencing poverty. Protected from discrimination by socio-economic equality laws and policies.

Emotional tax

The combination of being on guard to protect against bias, feeling different at work because of gender, race, and/or ethnicity, and the associated effects on health, well-being, and ability to thrive at work.

Enslaved person / People

A person or people whom has been forced into slavery against their will.

Ethnic Group

Refers to a group of people having a common heritage or ancestry, or a shared historical past, often with identifiable physical, cultural, linguistic and/or religious characteristics.

Ethnicity

A social construct which divides people into smaller social groups based on characteristics such as values, behavioral patterns, language, political and economic interests, history, and ancestral geographical base.

Ethnocentrism

The implied deviation from a supposed 'normal' when discussing race or culture. Avoid the terms 'non-white' and 'coloured' as these display white ethnocentrism – deviation from the supposed norm – which can obviously be offensive to black and minority ethnic people.

Equality

Evenly distributed access to resources and opportunity necessary for a safe and healthy life; uniform distribution of access that may or may not result in equitable outcomes.

Equal Opportunities

An explicit set of policies, guidelines and actions devised to eradicate discriminatory practices and to ensure access to and full participation in education and employment opportunities, housing, health care, and the services, goods and facilities available to the general community or offered by an organisation.

Equity

The guarantee of fair treatment, access, opportunity, and advancement for all. At the same time striving to identify and eliminate barriers that have prevented the full participation of some groups. The principle of equity acknowledges that there are historically underserved and underrepresented populations and that fairness regarding these unbalanced conditions is needed to assist equality in the provision of effective opportunities to all groups.

Eurocentrism

Presupposes the supremacy of Europe and Europeans in world culture and relates history according to a European perception and experience.

Faith

Used in this context as a person defining themselves to following a recognised and organised faith/religion or philosophy. They may or may not be active in that faith but the right to identification is theirs.

No Faith

A person whom identifies as having no religion or formalised belief. It does not always mean they are not spiritual and does not always mean they are atheists.

Faith/No Faith

A term used in equal opportunities to discuss people with and without a faith.

Faithism

The cultural, institutional and individual set of practices and beliefs that assign different values to people according to their religion or creed, or their lack of religion or creed, thereby resulting in differential treatment on the basis of faith.

FTM

A person transitioning from female to male.

Feminine

This is separate from gender and sex and focusing directly on the defining characteristics of femininity are not universally identical, some patterns
exist: gentleness, empathy, sensitivity, caring, sweetness, compassion, tolerance, nurturance, and deference, are traits that have traditionally been cited as feminine. Feminine behaviour, style and approach can be displayed by both Women and Men.

Feminism

The advocacy of Women's rights on the ground of the equality of the sexes.

Femme

Femme is a term used in LGBT community to describe someone who expresses themselves in a typically feminine way. Can often be found used as a derogatory word although for some it is becoming an empowering word.

G

Gay

A common and acceptable word for male homosexuals, but often used for both genders. It is normally only acceptable when discussing men or a man whom has romantic and/or sexual feelings towards other men or a man.

Gender

The socially constructed ideas about behaviour, actions, and roles a particular sex performs, acts and displays.

Gender binary

The viewpoint that gender consists of only two gender identities, male/female.

Gender dysphoria

Prolonged state of distress caused by one being uncomfortable identifying with the gender related to their assigned sex at birth. For instance, one can be born male, but is not comfortable identifying as a man.

Gender Identity

A personal conception of one's own gender; often in relation to a gender opposition between masculinity and femininity. It is how people externally communicate or perform their gender identity to others.

Gender Expression

An individual's outward and external gendered appearance. This may include, but in no way limited to, hair styles, clothes, accessories, and mannerisms. Gender expression may also include gender roles which are also defined by an individual's culture/society.

Gender fluid

A term depicting a person who does not identify with a single gender. Gender identity – One's concept of self as woman, man, blend of both, as two-spirit, or neither. One's gender identity may not be the same as one's assigned sex.

Gender non-conforming

A term for individuals whose gender identity does not fit into the societal expectations related to their assigned sex at birth.

Gender privilege

Gender privilege usually refers to male privilege, meaning a set of privileges granted to men on the basis of their gender.

Gender queer

Individuals who define their identify as neither entirely male nor entirely female.

Gender transition

The process a person goes through to live as the gender with which they identify, which is different from their assigned sex at birth.

Genetic Information

Genetic information includes information about an individual's genetic tests and the genetic tests of an individual's family members, as well as information about the manifestation of a disease or disorder in an individual's family members (i.e. family medical history).

Groupthink / Group Thinking

The practice of thinking or making decisions as a group in a way that discourages creativity or individual responsibility.

H

He-peating (aka man-peating)

A situation where a man appropriates or repeats a woman's comments or ideas and then is praised for them being his own.

Heterosexism

The perception that heterosexuality is superior to other sexual orientations.

Hetero-centic

Decision making or information which has been based or formulated on assumption with bias towards a Hetrosexual view of the world.

Heterosexual privilege

'Straight' privilege and cis-gendered privilege is the receiving of advantages that are favourably granted to someone solely because of their heterosexual orientation or the gender they identify with.

Homeless

Person experiencing homelessness.

Homophobia

The fear or hatred of people attracted to members of the same sex.

Homosexual

An adjective ascribed to individuals sexually attracted to individuals of the same sex. This term is now seen as outdated and offensive. Gay man/person/lesbian are preferred.

Human Rights

Base laws agreed upon by United Nations members that govern and guide all Equality, Diversity and Inclusion laws. These rights are intended to ensure everyone has a level of protection.

There are in fact 9 main international agreements that protect human rights:

- International Convention on the Elimination of All Forms of Racial Discrimination

- International Covenant on Civil and Political Rights

- International Covenant on Economic, Social and Cultural Rights

- Convention on the Elimination of All Forms of Discrimination against Women

- Convention against Torture and Other Cruel, Inhuman or Degrading Treatment or Punishment

- Convention on the Rights of the Child

- International Convention on Protection of the Rights of All Migrant Workers and Members of Their Families

- Universal Declaration of Human Rights

- The United Nations Convention on the Rights of the Child

- The Convention on the Rights of Persons with Disabilities

Humanitarian Action

Direct acts to save lives, alleviate suffering and maintain human dignity during and in the aftermath of man-made crises and natural disasters. It also aims to prevent and strengthen preparedness for when such situations occur. Humanitarian action are guided by the principles of humanity, impartiality, neutrality, and independence.

Humanitarian Setting

The space, both physical and emotional that direct action or the discussion of humanitarian action can take place.

Humankind

The preferred modern term over Mankind.

I

Implicit bias

(See Unconscious Bias) A biased which although an Unconscious Bias could be considered to have arose from laziness from the individual or organisation who have manifested the bias.

Immigrant

Those who move from their native country to another with the intention of settling for the purpose of forging a better life or for better opportunities. This may be for a variety of personal, political, religious, social or economic reasons. The word is sometimes used incorrectly to refer, implicitly or explicitly, to racialized peoples and to naturalized citizens.

Inclusion

The act of creating involvement, environments and empowerment in which any individual or group can be and feel welcomed, respected, supported, and valued to fully participate. An inclusive and welcoming climate with equal access to opportunities and resources embrace differences and offers respect in words and actions for all people.

Inclusive Leader

A form of leadership that intentionally welcomes and incorporates the contributions of all stakeholders within an organization to encourage teams to voice different perspectives, discuss difference of opinion, and inform the overall business strategy. Often using 'AGILE" style of facilitation management.

Inclusive Design

See Universal Design, a design approach to make a product, service or experience as close as possible to being accessible for all.

In-group bias

The tendency to respond more positively to people from our in-groups than we do to people from our outgroups.

Innate diversity

Innate Diversity is the range of differences in people like gender, age, race, physical ability and sexuality. It also includes differences in the way we think and process information.

Institutional Change

A planned approach to developing and implementing inclusive policies, programs and practices adapted to the needs of a diverse and evolving society.

Intercultural competence

The ability to develop targeted knowledge, skills and attitudes that lead to visible behaviour and communication that are both effective and appropriate in intercultural interactions.

Internally displaced people (IDPs)

People whom are refugees within their own country or otherwise forced to make journeys away from their homes due to catastrophe, humanitarian or natural disasters, climate change or poverty.

Intersectionality

The term intersectionality was coined by Black feminist scholar Kimberlé Crenshaw in 1989. "Intersectionality" represents an analytic framework that attempts to identify how interlocking systems of power impact those who are most marginalized in society.

Intersex

A term used for people born with reproductive or sexual anatomy and/or chromosome pattern that does not seem to fit typical definitions of male or female.

Imposter Syndrome

A psychological pattern in which an individual doubts their accomplishments and has a persistent internalized fear of being exposed as a "fraud".

L

Lesbian

A woman who is romantically and or sexually attracted to other women.

LGBT+

This is an accepted and inclusive way to represent all the different identities in the longer acronym.

Here is a breakdown of what each of the letters in LGBTQQIAAP mean:

- L - lesbian: a woman who is attracted to other women

- G - gay: a man who is attracted to other men or broadly people who identify as homosexual

- B - bisexual: a person who is attracted to both men and women

- T - transgender: a person whose gender identity is different or has changed from the sex the doctor put down on their birth certificate

- Q - queer: originally used as a hate term, some people want to reclaim the word, while others find it offensive. It can be a political statement, suggest that someone doesn't want to identify with "binaries" (e.g. male v female, homosexual v straight) or that they don't want to label themselves only by their sexual activity

- Q - questioning: a person who is still exploring their sexuality or gender identity

- I - intersex: a person whose body is not definitively male or female. This may be because they have chromosomes which are not XX or XY or because their genitals or reproductive organs are not considered "standard"

- A - allies: a person who identifies as straight but supports people in the LGBTQQIAAP community

- A - asexual: a person who is not attracted in a sexual way to people of any gender

- P - pansexual: a person whose sexual attraction is not based on gender and may themselves be fluid when it comes to gender or sexual identity.

Mansplain

Mainsplain is a combination of two words – "man" and "explain". Mansplaining refers to a man explaining something to someone, typically a woman, in a manner regarded as condescending or patronizing.

Masculine

This is separate from gender and sex and focusing directly on the defining characteristics of the fluid social construct of masculinity are not universally identical, some patterns exist: Energy, Forcefulness, Determination and strength are traits that have traditionally been cited as feminine. Masculine behaviour, style and approach can be displayed by both Women and Men.

Marginalisation

Treatment of a person, group or concept as insignificant or pervasive and places them outside of the mainstream society, government or an organization.

Mental health

The term referring to everyone's mental state or mental illness. We all have mental health, sometimes we are in good health, other times not, or we may be seeking treatment for improvement of health. It is best practice to recognise and reasonably adjust for, in the same way as a physical disability or physical illness.

Microaffirmations

Microaffirmations are subtle acknowledgments of a person's importance and accomplishments, which creates a feeling of being valued and a sense of belonging.

Micro-aggression(s)

Intentional or unintentional verbal, nonverbal or environmental slights/insults that communicate hostile, derogatory or negative messages to people based upon their marginalized group.

Minority

A term used to describe non-dominant social groups. Avoid using the term "minority", because it may imply an inferior social position.

Minority Group

Refers to a group of people within a society that is either small in numbers or that has little or no access to social, economic, political or religious power. Minority rights are protected by the UN Convention on the rights of minorities.

Models of Disability

The various right and wrong ways to think about and interact with Disabled People. The only acceptable and legally protected one is the Social Model of Disability.

MTF

A person transitioning from male to female.

Multiculturalism

The practice of acknowledging and respecting the various cultures, religions, languages, social equity, races, ethnicities, attitudes, and opinions within an environment. The theory and practice promote peaceful coexistence of all identities and people.

Multiracial, mixed heritage, dual heritage, mixed-race, mixed-ethnicity – or simply "mixed"

Terms describing a person who has parentage or ancestors from more than one ethnic and/or racial group. Some people can get confused between interracial and biracial. An individual may self describe as biracial if their heritage is mixed; interracial, on the other hand, is used to describe relationships or interactions between individuals from different racial groups.

N

Non-binary gender

Any gender that falls outside of the binary system of man/woman.

Non-disabled (Person)

The correct term for someone whom is not a Disabled Person.

Neurodiverse

Neurodiversity describes the spread of neurological differences (learning and developmental difficulties, ADHD and Autism are examples).

P

Peace

A concept of friendship, compassion and non-violent, non-aggressive solutions to interpersonal, personal, local, national and global issues.

Peace (Education)

Any project, initiative or education, formal or informal, which looks at ways to foster or provide tools for peace.

Person(s) / People of Colour

An outdated term based in ethnocentric ideas. Avoid its usage as it conveys a "White and People who are not white" generalist attitude.

Power

The ability to control, coerce or influence people based on privilege identities. Power may be positional and provide access to social, political, and economic resources.

Power (over)

When power is used in discriminatory and oppressive way. Having power over others and therefore domination and control over others (e.g. through coercion and violence) also exercising any privilege unduly or inconsiderately.

Power (sharing)

shared with all people in struggles for liberation and equality. Using or exercising one's power to work with others equitably, for example, in a social movement.

Prejudice

Refers to the (conscious or unconscious, positive or negative) attitudes and feelings one has towards an individual or group of individuals based on certain traits.

Privilege

Any and all unearned benefit, right or advantage an individual receives in society by nature of their identities, race, wealth and other characteristics.

Pronoun

Words we use to refer to people's gender in conversation – for example, 'he' or 'she'. Some people may prefer others to refer to them in gender-neutral language and use pronouns such as they/their and ze/zir.

Psychological Safety

Psychological safety, term coined and defined by Harvard Business School professor Amy Edmondson, is a belief that you will not be punished or humiliated for speaking up with ideas, questions, concerns or mistakes.

Objective justification

The term used to describe a justification for a specific role, service or appointment to be filled without equal opportunities. I.e. Where a person of a certain faith is required in a role discussing that faith.

Oppression

A state of being subject to unjust treatment or control either at the individual level or systematic level.

Outing

Exposing someone's gender identity or sexual orientation without that individual's permission.

Outgroup bias

The tendency to view people from outside our own group as less similar and, as a result, have negative biases against them.

Queer

Some LGBT+ people use this term as a way of reclaiming the power associated in the past with this term and other derogatory terms (such as fag or dyke). Others use it as a more general all-inclusive term to represent a variety of sexual orientations and/or gender identities or anything that defies easy definition or categorization. Like any term or label, there is no fixed view on what Queer means, and it is still considered offensive by some areas of the LGBT+ Community.

Race

A social construct that artificially divides people into distinct groups based on characteristics such as physical appearance, ancestral heritage, cultural affiliation, cultural history, ethnic classification, and the political needs of a society at a given point in time.

Racialisation

The process through which groups come to be socially constructed as races, based on characteristics such as race, ethnicity, language, economics, religion, culture, politics, etc. That is, treated outside the norm and receiving unequal treatment based upon phenotypical features.

Racism

Racism is any individual action, or institutional practice which treats people differently because of their colour or ethnicity. This distinction is often used to justify discrimination.

Rainbow Community

The multi-coloured rainbow flag was adopted in 1978 in San Francisco by the LGBTQ+ communities as a symbol of pride, solidarity, and the diversity of the gay community. The colours symbolize life (red), healing (orange), sunlight (yellow), nature (green), harmony/peace (blue), and spirit (purple violet).

Reasonable Adjustment

Adjustments for Disabled People to ensure all goods, services, jobs, and buildings are reasonably adjusted to ensure accessibility for as many people as possible or for an individual's needs.

Refugee

A person whom is currently stateless due to leaving their homes and countries for fear of their lives and wellbeing. A refugee is protected by various UN international conventions.

Religion

A Spiritual and/or cultural way of life for some people which helps to shape their ethical and world view point.

Respect

A feeling or understanding that someone or something is important, valued and should be treated in a dignified way.

S

Safe Space

A physical, theoretical or defined construct in which an individual can feel safe, secure and welcomed. This will vary between individuals and communities.

Sex

Classification of a person as male, female or intersex based on their reproductive organs and functions. Biological and physiological characteristics that define humans as female or male.

Sexual Orientation

The direction of one's sexual attraction toward the same gender, opposite gender, or other genders. It is on a continuum and not necessarily a set of absolute categories.

Sex reassignment surgery

Medical procedure altering one's physical appearance to further reflect one's gender identity.

Sizeism or Size discrimination

Discrimination based on a person's size. Size discrimination usually refers to extremes in physical size, such as very tall or short; extremely thin or fat. Like other forms of discrimination, sizeism isn't always explicit. It involves the perpetuation of stereotype and attitudes such as the idea that fat people are lazy, fat people eat too much and don't exercise which support those stereotypes, enough, tall people are good basketball players, or that overweight people often contract diseases which render some jobs dangerous for themselves and others. It is often seen as 'acceptable discrimination'.

Social Construct

An idea that appears to be natural and obvious to people who accept it but may or may not represent reality

Social Justice

To act as an advocate for a just society where all people have a right to fair and equitable treatment, support and resources.

Socioeconomic (privilege)

One or a set of advantages held by a person or group owing to their experience and their individual or family's social and economic status.

Socio-economic (status)

A person's status with regards to wealth and its potential negative impact if they have less.

Special Educational Needs (SEN)

An educational requirement for Schools to ensure fair, equal and safe access to education for Disabled People.

Specialised Education Needs

The preferred term for SEN requirements from the Disabled Community in the UK.

Special Needs

Outdated term for the requirements of a Disabled Person as part of a reasonable adjustment. Also used as a derogatory term.

Specialised Needs

Community preferred replacement term for Special Needs.

Stateless person

A person whom is a refugee, migrant or similar person existing without the support or recognition of a government state or country.

Stereotyping

The attribution of particular characteristics – appearance, temperament, potential etc.– to all members of an assumed group or 'race'. 'Race' is in fact a social and political construct rather than a biological one. Members of minority groups can sometimes be seen as deviant or threatening and subsequently stereotyped with negative characteristics – laziness or criminality for example. Even 'benign' stereotyping – as in the notions that all Asians are ambitious or that Muslim girls are passive – can be misleading and damaging.

Stereotype threat

A situational predicament in which people are or feel themselves to be at risk of conforming to stereotypes about their social group.

Straight

Refers to a person who is emotionally, romantically, and/or physically attracted to someone of the opposite sex. The term Heterosexual is often preferred.

Sustainable Development Goals (SDGs)

The 17 Goals which every world government has signed up to assist deliver with key global partners to create a more sustainable and equitable world.

The 17 sustainable development goals (SDGs) to transform our world:

GOAL 1: No Poverty

GOAL 2: Zero Hunger

GOAL 3: Good Health and Well-being

GOAL 4: Quality Education

GOAL 5: Gender Equality

GOAL 6: Clean Water and Sanitation

GOAL 7: Affordable and Clean Energy

GOAL 8: Decent Work and Economic Growth

GOAL 9: Industry, Innovation and Infrastructure

GOAL 10: Reduced Inequality

GOAL 11: Sustainable Cities and Communities

GOAL 12: Responsible Consumption and Production

GOAL 13: Climate Action

GOAL 14: Life Below Water

GOAL 15: Life on Land

GOAL 16: Peace and Justice Strong Institutions

GOAL 17: Partnerships to achieve the Goal

Systemic Discrimination

The institutionalisation of discrimination through policies and practices which may appear neutral on the surface, but which have an exclusionary impact on particular groups, such that various minority groups are discriminated against, intentionally or unintentionally. This occurs in institutions and organizations where the policies, practices and procedures (e.g. employment systems – job requirements, hiring practices, promotion procedures, etc.) exclude and/or act as barriers to some groups. Systemic discrimination may also result from some government laws and regulations. This can be the result of an unconscious bias.

"To be out"

To be open about your sexual orientation and/or your gender identity.

Transgender

An umbrella term for transsexuals, cross-dressers (transvestites), gender queers, and people who identify as neither female nor male and/or as neither a man nor as a woman. Transgender is not a sexual orientation; transgender people may have any sexual orientation.

Transgender people are those whose psychological self ("gender identity" – one's internal experience of their gender) differs from the physical sex with which they were born ("biological sex" - one's body -genitals, chromosomes, etc.). Often, society conflates sex and gender, viewing them as the same thing. However, gender and sex are not the same thing.

continued over

The term 'Trans' is often used as shorthand for Transgender.

Transgender man

The term for a transgender individual who identifies as a man (or whose gender identity is of a man) and was assigned female at birth.

Transgender woman

The term for a transgender individual who identifies as a woman (or whose gender identity is of a woman) and was assigned male at birth.

Transphobia

The fear or hatred of transgender individuals.

Transsexual

The term for a person whose gender identity is different from the assigned sex at birth, and who may alter his/her/their body through clothing, cosmetics, hormones and in some cases surgery to be more in line with their gender identity.

Trans-Exclusionary-Radical-Feminists (TERFs)

A term coined to discuss the rise of Trans-Exclusionary sentiment by some women. Although term is unpopular with the community as it links to feminism negatively it is a used umbrella term for this biased viewpoint.

Travellers

Romany Gypsies and Irish Travellers are defined as ethnic groups and protected from discrimination under the UK Equality Act 20104. With an estimated population of between two and twenty million Gypsies in Europe, they constitute the largest ethnic minority group on the continent.

There are a number of different groups who fall under the title of Gypsies and Travellers; Romany Gypsies, Irish Travellers, Scottish Gypsies and Travellers, Welsh Gypsies and Travellers, New Travellers, Bargees and others living in cruising boats and Travelling Show-people.

Two-Spirit

The term used in some communities to describe person whose individual spirit is a combination of both male and female spirits.

Unconscious Bias

Your background, personal experiences, societal stereotypes and cultural context can have an impact on your decisions and actions without you realising. Implicit or unconscious bias happens by our brains making incredibly quick judgments and assessments of people and situations without us realising.

Underrepresented/Underserved/Marginalised

Individuals, communities or groups that have historically been or currently are inadequately or insufficiently represented, under resourced, and/or oppressed due to structural and/or societal obstacles and disparities.

Underrepresented groups

Refers to a group whose members are disadvantaged and subjected to unequal treatment by the dominant group, and who may regard themselves as recipients of collective discrimination.

Universal or Inclusive Design

Designing products, instructional materials, services and spaces so that the widest possible range of people can use them. Universal Design evolved from Accessible or Barrier Free Design, a process that addresses the needs of people with disabilities. Universal Design goes further by recognizing that there is a wide spectrum of human abilities. Everyone, even the most able-bodied person, passes through childhood, periods of temporary illness, injury and old age. By designing for this human diversity, the focus is on creating an environment (physical, learning and service) that is easier for all people to use.

Visually impaired

The correct term for a person whom is blind or has a visual impairment or disability. Never use the term 'Blind Person' unless an individual you are communicating with has stated this as a preference.

Visual Tracking

A name given to common visual impairments where the eye can be thrown off from information accessing due to colour, type or patterning within the design. Becoming a major access requirement for Smartphones and Online Media.

Visual Aphasia

A term sometimes used with certain colour-blind, epilepsy or other minor conditions where combinations of colour within a design or document conspire to cause temporary blindness or 'fitting' due to it's nature. A high profile example of this is the London 2012 Olympic logo launch.

W

Wheelchair user

The correct term for a Disabled Person whom uses a wheelchair either constantly, frequently or occasionally.

White

A social colour. The term is used to refer to people belonging to the majority group in the UK and Europe. It is recognized that there are many different people who are "White" but who face discrimination because of their class, gender, ethnicity, religion, age, language, or geographical origin. Grouping these people as "White" is not to deny the very real forms of discrimination that people of certain ancestry, such as Italian, Portuguese, Jewish, Armenian, Greek, etc., face because of these factors.

White privilege

The unquestioned and unearned set of advantages and benefits bestowed on people solely because they are white. Often people with this privilege can be unaware of it as these privileges are perpetuated systemically across institutions including in the law, work, medicine, and more.

White supremacy (thinking)

A cultural thinking pattern which can be challenged; For instance, equating white with civilised or best, black with backward or of less worth.

Workplace inclusion

An atmosphere where all employees belong, contribute and can thrive. It requires deliberate and intentional action.

X

Xenophobia

Dislike of or prejudice against people from other countries or cultures.

Z

Zero sum-game

The idea that if one person gains something, another person loses something. When doing 'EDI' work, sometimes dominant groups believe that an organisation helps make underrepresented groups feel more included, they lose power, influence, and privilege.

UNITED NATIONS SUSTAINABLE DEVELOPMENT GOALS (SDGs)

A world first for humanity. The 17 Goals were agreed by all United Nations Member States in 2015. They provide a shared global plan for peace and prosperity for people and the planet, now and into the future.

There are 17 Sustainable Development Goals (SDGs), which are an urgent call for action by all countries - developed and developing - in a global partnership.

They recognise that ending poverty, enabling Gender Equality and overcoming inequalities and many other deprivations must go hand-in-hand with strategies that improve health and education, and spur economic growth – all while tackling climate change and working to preserve our oceans and forests.

The goals all have sub-goals and aims which allow humanity to work collectively, locally to effect global change. The COVID-19 Pandemic highlighted in many countries where inequalities are. Throwing the stark contrast between privileges to the forefront. By working to this simple 17 Goal plan we can ensure that as the world changes, moves forward and becomes more inter-connected that no one is left behind.

In all the Equality, Diversity, Inclusion, or Human Rights planning we do it is important we recognise these goals and work towards them. This book for instance meets multiple goals at one time. Which is vitally important, as you must work in a matrix approach not just focusing on a singular goal as by doing so you are missing opportunities to include more viewpoints and increase diversity of ideas.

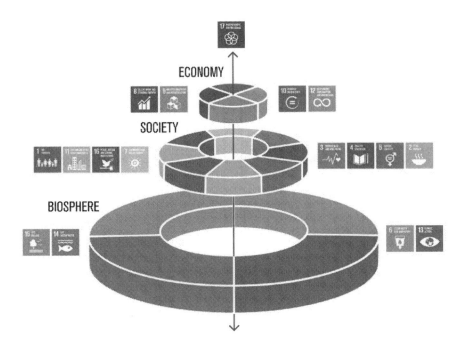

This inter-connectivity of all things is at the heart of the SDGs, with an aim to achieve a balance of Environment, Planet and Biosphere, Societies and Communities and Economies.

For further information on the Sustainable Development Goals please try out the following websites:

United Nations Sustainable Development:

sustainabledevelopment.un.org

Scouts for SDGs (Youth engagement)

sdgs.scout.org

There is also a wide range of resources available on YouTube.

For Equality, Diversity and Inclusion interests I would strongly recommend exploring the hashtags:

#LeaveNoOneBehind

#SDG10   #SDG5 #SDG4

Diversity Calendar

January

1st New Year's Day - Start of the Gregorian Calendar

4th International Braille Day (UN)

9th World Religion Day

23rd International Day of Education (UN)

27th International Day of Commemoration in Memory of the Victims of the Holocaust (UN)

February

LGBT+ History Month UK

2nd Groundhog Day

6th Time to Talk Day (UK)
International Day of Zero tolerance of Female Genital Mutilation (UN)

20th World Day of Social Justice

21st International Mother Language Day (UN)

March

Jewish History Month

1st St David's Day - Patron Saint of Wales UK

Zero Discrimination Day (UN)

8th International Women's Day (UN)

17th St Patrick's Day - Patron Saint of Ireland

20th International Day of Happiness (UN)

French Language Day (UN)

21st International Day for the elimination of Racial Discrimination (UN)

International Day of NOWRUZ (UN)

International Down Syndrome Day (UN)

World Poetry Day

22nd World Water Day (UN)

24th World Tuberculoses Day (WHO)

International Day for the right to the truth concerning Gross Human
Rights Violations and for the dignity of victims (UN)

25th International Day of Remembrance of the Victims of Slavery and
the Transatlantic Slave Trade (UN)

31st International Transgender Day of Visibility

April

Stress awareness month (UK & USA)

1st April Fools Day

2nd World Autism Awareness Day

4th International Day of Landmine Awareness and Assistance in Mine Action (UN)

5th International Day of Conscience (UN)

6th International Day of Sport for the Development of Peace (UN)

7th World Health Day (WHO)

12th International Day of Human Space Flight (UN)

20th Holocaust Remembrance Day - from sunset
International Chinese Language Day (UN)

21st Holocaust Remembrance Day - to nightfall
World Creativity and Innovation Day

23rd World Book Day
World English Language Day
World Spanish Language Day
International Girls in ICT Day (UN)

24th International Day of Multilateralism
and Dialogue for Peace Day (UN)

26th International Chernobyl Disaster Remembrance Day (UN)

28th World Safety and Health at Work Day

May

1st May day (UK)

3rd World Press Freedom Day

15th International Day of Families (UN)

16th International Day of Living together in Peace (UN)

17th International Day Against Homophobia, Transphobia and Biphobia

Mental Health Awareness Week

20th World Bee Day

21st International Tea Day (UN)
World Day for Cultural Diversity for Dialogue and Development

23rd International Day to End Obstetric Fistula (UN)

28th Shavuot Starts

29th International Day of UN Peace Keeping (UN)

30th Shavuot Ends

June

LGBT+ Pride Month UK

1st Global Day of Parents

3rd World Bicycle Day

4th International Day of Innocent Children Victims of Aggression (UN)

5th World Environment Day

6th Russian Language Day

7th World Food Safety Day

8th World Oceans Day

12th World Day Against Child Labour

13th Albinism Awareness Day (UN)

14th World Blood Donor Day

National Refugee Week

15th World Elder Abuse Awareness Day

16th International Day of Family Remittances (Economic Migrants)(UN)

19th Inter. Day for the Elimination of Sexual Violence in Conflict (UN)

20th World Refugee Day

21st International Day of Yoga (UN)
International Day of the Celebration of the Solstice (UN)

23rd International Widows Day (UN)

25th Day of the Sea-fairer

July

4ʰ International Day of Cooperatives (UN)

11ᵗʰ World Population Day

15ᵗʰ World Youth Skills Day

18ᵗʰ Nelson Mandela International Day

30ᵗʰ International Day of Friendship (UN)
World Day against Human Trafficking

August

9th International Day of the Worlds Indigenous People (UN)

12th International Youth Day (UN)

19th World Humanitarian Day

21st International Day of Remembrance and Tribute to the Victims of Terrorism (UN)

22nd International Day Commemorating the Victims of Acts of Violence based on Religion or Belief (UN)

23rd International for the Remembrance of the Slave trade (UN)

30th International Day for the Victims in forced disappearances (UN)

September

5th International Day of Charity (UN)

7th International Day for Clean Air for Blue Skies (UN)

8th International Literacy Day (UN)

17th World Patient Safety Day

18th International Equal Pay Day (UN)

21st International Day of Peace (UN)

23rd International Day of Sign Languages (UN)

24th World Maritime Day

28th International Day of Universal Access to Information (UN)

30th International Translation Day (UN)

October

Black History Month (UK)

1st International Day of Older Persons (UN)

2nd International Day of Non-Violence (UN)

5th World Teachers Day

9th World Post Day

10th World Mental Health Day

11th International Day of the Girl (UN)

15th International Day of Rural Women (UN)

16th World Food Day

17th International Day of the Eradication of Poverty (UN)

27th World Day for Audiovisual Heritage

31st World Cities Day

November

Disability History Months (UK)

10th World Science Day for Peace

15th World Remembrance Day for Road Traffic Victims

16th International Day for Tolerance (UN)

19th World Toilet Day
World Philosophy Day

20th World Children's Day

21st World Television Day

25th International day of the Elimination of the Violence Against Women (UN)

30th International Day of Remembrance for all Victims of Chemical Warfare

December

Disability History Months (UK)

1st World AIDS Day

2nd International Day of the Abolition of Slavery (UN)

3rd International Day of Persons with Disabilities (UN)

5th Inter. Volunteer Day for Economic & Social Development (UN)

10th Human Rights Day

18th International Migrants Day (UN)
Arabic Language Day

20th International Human Solidarity Day (UN)

Faith / No Faith Introduction Guide

An introductory guide to terminology, customs and people from different faiths and beliefs. This is a non-exhaustive selection of key world faith and intended as a brief guide to ensure a base level knowledge before learning more by interaction with people from the community.

People of No Faith

People who believe that god or gods (or other supernatural beings) are man-made constructs, myths and legends or who believe that these concepts are not meaningful.
They may still have a spiritual outlook.

This includes:

- Atheism

- Humanism

- Postmodernism

- Rationalism

- Secularism

- Unitarian

- Universalism

Ceremonies

People often mark the major life stage events in life - like being born, getting married and so on - with religious ceremonies like christenings, weddings and funerals.

Atheist and Humanist organisations offer their own rituals for these events that give them meaning and significance without any religious content. Such as Naming Ceremonies, Weddings, and Funerals.

These ceremonies differ from mainstream secular ceremonies like civil weddings, in that they are highly personalised for the individuals concerned.

Key people

Humanist organisations train people to officiate at humanist ceremonies, and compile lists of those who are qualified to do so.

Bahá'í

The Bahá'í faith is one of the youngest of the world's major religions. It was founded by Bahá'u'lláh in Iran in 1863.

Iran was then mainly a Muslim country, and the faith was proclaimed by a young Iranian, who called himself The Báb. He said that a messenger would soon arrive from God, who would be the latest in a line of prophets including Moses, Muhammad and Jesus Christ.

Bahá'u'lláh, which means the Glory of God in Arabic, was born Mirza Husayn Ali in 1817. Bahá'í's believe that Bahá'u'lláh is the most recent Manifestation of God. Bahá'u'lláh himself stated that he is not God's final messenger

The Bahá'í faith accepts all religions as having true and valid origins. The idea of progressive revelation is of central significance for the Bahá'í faith. Bahá'u'lláh taught that God intervenes throughout human history at different times to reveal more of himself through his messengers (called Divine Messengers, or Manifestations of God)

The central idea of the faith is that of unity. They believe that people should work together for the common benefit of humanity

There are 6 million Bahá'ís in the world, in 235 countries and around 6,000 live in Britain.

Bahá'í worship

Bahá'ís see themselves as a people with a mission to bring harmony and unity in the world, and this is reflected in their spiritual practice.

The main purpose of life for Bahá'ís is to know and love God.

Prayer, fasting and meditation are the main ways of achieving this and for making spiritual progress.

Service to others is worship

Bahá'í texts state that work performed in the spirit of service to humanity is a form of worship.

Worship meeting in a large, light room with chairs arranged around a central speaker.

Absence of ritual

The Bahá'í faith has no clergy or sacraments, and virtually no rituals.

The three Bahá'í rituals:

- Obligatory daily prayers

- Reciting the prayer for the dead at a funeral

- The simple marriage rite

There are two reasons Bahá'ís avoid ritual:

Rituals can easily degenerate and become meaningless, so that people carry them out for the sake of the ritual and forget the spiritual purpose behind them.

Rituals can be a form of cultural imperialism, imposing the same rituals across different cultures and destroying their rich diversity

Events and celebrations

Doing without rituals does not mean doing without celebrations or special events.

Communal worship

Bahá'ís have no liturgy, since the minimising of ritual makes it impossible to develop one. The emphasis on prayer and meditation, and on social action in Bahá'í thinking means that congregational worship plays a much smaller part in Bahá'í life than it does in other faiths.

A typical Bahá'í temple: striking tiered, domed building of white stone

Bahá'í services are very simple with readings from the scriptures, along with interpretations of them and prayers. Hymns and poetry are allowed, but not common. The atmosphere is usually dignified.

Bahá'í are encouraged to come together in communal worship, but there are no congregational prayers. One person will recite prayers on behalf of everyone present.

This is because prayer is seen essentially as a private duty, and because there are no professional clergy within the Bahá'í faith.

Morning prayer

Bahá'í scripture recommends that the community should meet together for prayer each morning, although this is not commonly done by modern Bahá'ís.

Nineteen day feast

For modern Bahá'í the main occasion for group worship is the devotional portion of the nineteen day feast.

Holy days

Bahá'ís usually hold special worship events on holy days and festivals.

Buddhism

Buddhism is a spiritual tradition that focuses on personal spiritual development and the attainment of a deep insight into the true nature of life. There are 376 million followers worldwide. It is important to realise Buddhism is not a religion but considered a philosophy.

Buddhists seek to reach a state of nirvana or assist all life to reach this state. Following the path of the Buddha, Siddhartha Gautama, who went on a quest for Enlightenment around the sixth century BC.

There is no belief in a personal god. Buddhists believe that nothing is fixed or permanent and that change is always possible. The path to Enlightenment is through the practice and development of morality, meditation and wisdom.

Buddhists believe that life is both endless and subject to impermanence, suffering and uncertainty. These states are called the tilakhana, or the three signs of existence. Existence is endless because individuals are reincarnated over and over again, experiencing suffering throughout many lives.

It is impermanent because no state, good or bad, lasts forever. Our mistaken belief that things can last is a chief cause of suffering.

The Buddha

Siddhartha Gautama, the Buddha, was born into a royal family in present-day Nepal over 2500 years ago. He lived a life of privilege and luxury until one day he left the royal enclosure and encountered for the first time, an old man, a sick man, and a corpse. Disturbed by this he became a monk before adopting the harsh poverty of Indian asceticism. Neither path satisfied him and he decided to pursue the 'Middle Way' - a life without luxury but also without poverty.

Buddhists believe that one day, seated beneath the Bodhi tree (the tree of awakening), Siddhartha became deeply absorbed in meditation and reflected on his experience of life until he became enlightened.

By finding the path to enlightenment, Siddhartha was led from the pain of suffering and rebirth towards the path of enlightenment and became known as the Buddha or 'awakened one'.

Schools of Buddhism

There are numerous different schools or sects of Buddhism. The two largest are Theravada Buddhism, which is most popular in Sri Lanka, Cambodia, Thailand, Laos and Burma (Myanmar), and Mahayana Buddhism, which is strongest in Tibet, China, Taiwan, Japan, Korea, and Mongolia.

Buddhist do not seek to proselytise -preach and convert.

All schools of Buddhism seek to aid followers on a path of enlightenment.

Key facts

- Buddhism is 2,500 years old

- There are currently 376 million followers worldwide

- There are over 150,000 Buddhists in Britain

- Buddhism arose as a result of Siddhartha Gautama's quest for Enlightenment in around the 6th CenturyBC

- There is no belief in a personal God. It is not centred

on the relationship between humanity and God

- Buddhists believe that nothing is fixed or permanent - change is always possible

- The two main Buddhist sects are Theravada Buddhism and Mahayana Buddhism, but there are many more

- Buddhists can worship both at home or at a temple

- The path to Enlightenment is through the practice and development of morality, meditation and wisdom.

Buddhist worship

Buddhists can worship both at home or at a temple. It is not considered essential to go to a temple to worship with others, but do require access to a Buddhist teacher, -a Master or Lama depending on traditions.

At home

Buddhists will often set aside a room or a part of a room as a shrine. There will be a statue of Buddha, candles, and an incense burner.

Temples

Buddhist temples come in many shapes. Perhaps the best known are the pagodas of China and Japan. Another typical Buddhist building is the Stupa, which is a stone structure built over what are thought to be relics of the Buddha, or over copies of the Buddha's teachings.

All Buddhist temples contain an image or a statue of Buddha.

Worship/Practice

There are as many forms of Buddhist practice as there are schools of Buddhism - and there are many of those.

Worship in Mahayana tradition takes the form of devotion to Buddha and to Bodhisattvas.

Buddhists may sit on the floor barefoot facing an image of Buddha and chanting. They will listen to monks chanting from religious texts, perhaps accompanied by instruments, and take part in meditations.

There is no western idea of prayer in Buddhism, rather a meditation state to connect with the Buddha and Bodhisattvas to celebrate them as teachers and also learn better ways to live and gain enlightenment.

Mantras and Meditations

Mantras

A mantra is a word, a syllable, a phrase or a short prayer that is spoken once or repeated over and over again (either aloud or in a person's head) and that is thought to have a profound spiritual effect on the person.

A very well known mantra is the mantra of Avalokiteshvara: 'om mani padme hum'.

Physical prayer aids

It's common to use mala beads to mark the number of repetitions of a mantra.

Mantras may also be displayed on a prayer wheel and repeated by spinning the wheel, or written on a prayer flag - in which case the prayer is repeated each time the flag moves in the wind.

Prayer wheels can be tiny things that a Buddhist carries with them or enormous objects up to nine feet high found in monasteries.

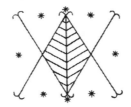

Candomblé

Candomblé is a religion based on African beliefs which is particularly popular in Brazil. It is also practised in many other countries and has as many as two million followers.

The religion is a blend of Yoruba, Fon and Bantu beliefs which originated from different regions in Africa. It has also incorporated some aspects of the Catholic faith over time.

Enslaved Africans brought their beliefs with them when they were shipped to Brazil during the slave trade.

The name Candomblé means 'dance in honour of the gods'.

Practitioners of Candomblé believe in one all powerful God called Oludumaré who is served by lesser deities. These deities are called orixas. (They can also be called voduns and inkices.)

Candomblé practitioners believe that every person has their own individual orixa which controls his or her destiny and acts as a protector.

Music and dance are important parts of Candomblé ceremonies. Specially choreographed dances are performed by worshippers to enable them to become possessed by the orixas.

There is no concept of good or bad in Candomblé. Each person is only required to fulfil his or her destiny to the fullest, regardless of what that is.

Candomblé is an oral tradition and therefore has no holy scriptures.

Places of worship

Historically worship services used to be held in the homes of the enslaved. There is an important distinction between sacred and profane places for Candomblécists. In profane places, ordinary everyday life occurs; work, play, relaxation and eating.

Sacred places are called terreiro or temples. They are buildings with indoor and outdoor spaces, and special areas for the gods.

Worshippers wear clean clothes and splash water on themselves before they enter to rid themselves of the uncleanliness of the world.

Followers go to terreiro for a number of reasons. Many go to have their fortunes told. To do this, a priest or priestess casts cowry shells and interprets the pattern in which they fall. Others go for months to immerse themselves in the spiritual and become possessed by their orixa.

Women in Candomblé

Women are very important in the Candomblé faith. Services are usually led by women, called 'mothers of the holy one', and it is the women who are responsible for ensuring the training of future priestesses.

Dance during worship

Worship takes the form of specially choreographed dances and hymns. The dance is a call to the spirits. At its height, the worshipper's orixa temporarily possesses the dancer's body and he or she enters into a trance like state and dances alone. Finally the gods are expelled. This is done by singing the hymns again, but in reverse order starting with the last hymn.

African dancing was well known to the slave owners. Even though the dance as a form of worship was forbidden, the enslaved would still dance in their free time in the fields.

These dances became important symbols of rebellion. Their rhythmic movements and rocking bodies belied the truth behind the dances. The enslaved Africans practised a form of martial art within the dances, seamlessly moving from attacking positions to defensive ones, learning to quickly gauge how to react to their opponent. This dance is called capoeira and has become increasingly popular in the West as an art form.

Christianity

Christianity is the most popular religion in the world with over 2 billion adherents. 42 million Britons see themselves as nominally Christian, and there are 6 million who are actively practising.

Key facts

- Christians believe that Jesus was the Messiah promised in the Old Testament.

- Christians believe that Jesus Christ is the Son of God.

- Christians believe that God sent his Son to earth to save humanity from the consequences of its sins.

- One of the most important concepts in Christianity is that of Jesus giving his life on the Cross (the Crucifixion) and rising from the dead on the third day (the Resurrection).

- Christians believe that there is only one God, but that there are three elements to this one God:

- God the Father

- God the Son

- The Holy Spirit

- Christians worship in churches.

- Their spiritual leaders are called priests or ministers.

- The Christian holy book is the Bible, and consists of the Old and New Testaments.

Christian holy days such as Easter and Christmas are important milestones in the Western secular calendar

Christian worship

Christian worship involves praising God in music and speech, readings from scripture, prayers of various sorts, a sermon, and various holy ceremonies (often called sacraments) such as the Eucharist.

While worship is often thought of only as services in which Christians come together in a group, individual Christians can worship God on their own, and in any place.

Origins

Christian worship grew out of Jewish worship. Jesus Christ was a religious Jew who attended the synagogue and celebrated Jewish festivals, and his disciples were familiar with Jewish ritual and tradition.

The first obvious divergence from Judaism was making Sunday the holy day instead of Saturday. By doing this the day of Christian worship is the same as the day that Jesus rose from the dead.

Jesus's promise to stay with his followers, fulfilled in the sending of the Holy Spirit, illuminated the development of Christian worship from early times.

So Christians regard worship as something that they don't only do for God, but that God, through Jesus's example and the presence of the Holy Spirit is also at work in.

Church services

Church services on a Sunday divide into two general types: Eucharistic services and services of the Word. Both types of service will include hymns, readings and prayers.

The Eucharistic service will be focussed on the act of Holy Communion.

The service of the Word does not include this rite, but instead features a much longer sermon, in which the preacher will speak at length to expound a biblical text and bring out its relevance to those present.

Different churches, even within the same denomination, will use very different styles of worship. Some will be elaborate, with a choir singing difficult music, others will hand the music over to the congregation, who sing simpler hymns or worship songs. Some churches leave much of the action to the minister, while others encourage great congregational participation.

Subdivisions and Denominations

The following highlights some of the many different ways in which Christians celebrate their faith:

- The Amish

- Baptist churches

- Christadelphians

- Church of England

- Church of Scotland

- Coptic Orthodox Church

- Eastern Orthodox Church

- Exclusive Brethren

- Methodist Church

- Opus Dei

- Pentecostalism

- Quakers Roman

- Catholic Church

- Salvation Army

- Seventh-day Adventists

- United Reformed Church

- Church of Africa

- Evangelicals Church

Hinduism

Hinduism is the religion of the majority of people in India and Nepal. It also exists among significant populations outside of the sub-continent and has over 900 million adherents worldwide.

In some ways Hinduism is the oldest living religion in the world, or at least elements within it stretch back many thousands of years. Yet Hinduism resists easy definition partly because of the vast array of practices and beliefs found within it. It is also closely associated conceptually and historically with the other Indian religions Jainism, Buddhism and Sikhism.

Unlike most other religions, Hinduism has no single founder, no single scripture, and no commonly agreed set of teachings. Throughout its extensive history, there have been many key figures teaching different philosophies and writing numerous holy books. For these reasons, writers often refer to Hinduism as 'a way of life' or 'a family of religions' rather than a single religion.

Defining Hinduism

The term 'Hindu' was derived from the river or river complex of the northwest, the Sindhu. Sindhu is a Sanskrit word used by the inhabitants of the region, the Aryans in the second millennium BCE. Later migrants and invaders, the Persians in the sixth century BCE, the Greeks from the 4th century BCE, and the Muslims from the 8th century CE, used the name of this river in their own languages for the land and its people.

The term 'Hindu' itself probably does not go back before the 15th and 16th centuries when it was used by people to differentiate themselves from followers of other traditions, especially the Muslims (Yavannas), in Kashmir and Bengal. At that time the term may have simply indicated groups united by certain cultural practices such as cremation of the dead and styles of cuisine. The 'ism' was added to 'Hindu' only in the 19th century in the context of British colonialism and missionary activity.

The origins of the term 'hindu' are thus cultural, political and geographical. Now the term is widely accepted although any definition is subject to much debate. In some ways it is true to say that Hinduism is a religion of recent origin, yet its roots and formation go back thousands of years.

Some claim that one is 'born a Hindu', but there are now many Hindus of non-Indian descent. Others claim that its core feature is belief in an impersonal Supreme, but important strands have long described and worshipped a personal God. Outsiders often criticise Hindus as being polytheistic, but many adherents claim to be monotheists.

Some Hindus define orthodoxy as compliance with the teachings of the Vedic texts (the four Vedas and their supplements). However, still others identify their tradition with 'Sanatana Dharma', the eternal order of conduct that transcends any specific body of sacred literature. Scholars sometimes draw attention to the caste system as a defining feature, but many Hindus view such practices as merely a social phenomenon or an aberration of their original teachings. Nor can we define Hinduism according to belief in concepts such as karma and samsara (reincarnation) because Jains, Sikhs, and Buddhists (in a qualified form) accept this teaching too.

Although it is not easy to define Hinduism, we can say that it is rooted in India, most Hindus revere a body of texts as sacred scripture known as the Veda, and most Hindus draw on a common system of values known as dharma.

Key Facts

- About 80% of the Indian population regard themselves as Hindu.

- Most Hindus believe in a Supreme God, whose qualities and forms are represented by the multitude of deities which emanate from him.

- Hindus believe that existence is a cycle of birth, death, and rebirth, governed by Karma.

- Hindus believe that the soul passes through a cycle of successive lives and its next incarnation is always dependent on how the previous life was lived.

- The main Hindu texts are the Vedas and their supplements (books based on the Vedas). Veda is a Sanskrit word meaning 'knowledge'. These scriptures do not mention the word 'Hindu' but many scriptures discuss dharma, which can be rendered as 'code of conduct', 'law', or 'duty'

- Hindus celebrate many holy days, but the Festival of Lights, Diwali is the best known.

- The 2001 census recorded 559,000 Hindus in Britain.

Puja (Worship)

Hindu worship, or puja, involves images (murtis), prayers (mantras) and diagrams of the universe (yantras).

Central to Hindu worship is the image, or icon, which can be worshipped either at home or in the temple.

Hindu worship is primarily an individual act rather than a communal one, as it involves making personal offerings to the deity.

Worshippers repeat the names of their favourite gods and goddesses, and repeat mantras. Water, fruit, flowers and incense are offered to god.

Worship at home

The majority of Hindu homes have a shrine where offerings are made, and prayers are said. A shrine can be anything: a room, a small altar or simply pictures or statues of the deity.

Family members often worship together. Rituals should strictly speaking be performed three times a day. Some Hindus, but not all, worship wearing the sacred thread (over the left shoulder and hanging to the right hip). This is cotton for the Brahmin (priest), hemp for the Kshatriya (ruler) and wool for the vaishya (merchants).

Temple worship

At a Hindu temple, different parts of the building have a different spiritual or symbolic meaning.

The central shrine is the heart of the worshipper

The tower represents the flight of the spirit to heaven

A priest may read, or more usually recite, the Vedas to the assembled worshippers, but any "twice-born" Hindu can perform the reading of prayers and mantras

Religious rites

Hindu religious rites are classified into three categories:

- Nitya rituals are performed daily and consist in offerings made at the home shrine or performing puja to the family deities.

- Naimittika rituals are important but only occur at certain times during the year, such as celebrations of the festivals, thanksgiving and so on.

- Kamya are rituals which are "optional" but highly desirable. Pilgrimage is one such.

Pilgrimage

Pilgrimage is an important aspect of Hinduism. It's an undertaking to see and be seen by the deity. Popular pilgrimage places are rivers, but temples, mountains, and other sacred sites in India are also destinations for pilgrimages, as sites where the gods may have appeared or become manifest in the world.

Kumbh Mela

Once every 12 years, up to 10 million people share in ritual bathing at the Kumbh Mela festival at Allahabad where the waters of the Ganges and Jumna combine. Hindus from all walks of life gather there for ritual bathing, believing that their sins will be washed away. The bathing is followed by spiritual purification which gains the blessings of the deity.

River Ganges

The river Ganges is the holiest river for Hindus.

Varanasi

This city, also known as Benares, is situated on the banks of the Ganges and is one of the most important pilgrimage centres. A Hindu who dies at Varanasi and has their ashes scattered on the Ganges is said to have experienced the best death possible.

Islam

The word Islam means 'submission to the will of God'.

Islam is the second largest religion in the world with over 1 billion followers. The 2001 census recorded 1,591,000 Muslims in the UK, around 3% of the population.

Key Facts

- Muslims believe that Islam was revealed over 1400 years ago in Mecca, Arabia.

- Followers of Islam are called Muslims.

- Muslims believe that there is only One God.

- The Arabic word for God is Allah.

- According to Muslims, God sent a number of prophets to mankind to teach them how to live according to His law.

- Jesus, Moses and Abraham are respected as prophets of God.

- They believe that the final Prophet was Muhammad.

- Muslims believe that Islam has always existed, but for practical purposes, date their religion from the time of the migration of Muhammad.

- Muslims base their laws on their holy book the Qur'an, and the Sunnah.

- Muslims believe the Sunnah is the practical example of Prophet Muhammad and that there are five basic Pillars of Islam.

- These pillars are the declaration of faith, praying five times a day, giving money to charity, fasting and a pilgrimage to Mecca (at least once).

Worship

Although Muslims can pray to God at any time, there are five prayers they are obligated to perform throughout the day.

They follow the same pattern so everyone can follow in congregation, and set prayers are always recited in Arabic.

Takbir is entering into the state of prayer by glorifying God. Muslims face towards Makkah and make the intention to pray. To begin the act of prayer, they say 'Allahu Akbar' meaning God is great, raising the hands to the ears or shoulder.

The Five Pillars of Islam

The most important Muslim practices are the Five Pillars of Islam. The five obligations that every Muslim must satisfy in order to live a good and responsible life according to Islam.

The Five Pillars consist of:

- Shahadah: sincerely reciting the Muslim profession of faith

- Salat: performing ritual prayers in the proper way five times each day

- Zakat: paying an alms (or charity) tax to benefit the poor and the needy

- Sawm: fasting during the month of Ramadan

- Hajj: pilgrimage to Mecca

Carrying out these obligations provides the framework of a Muslim's life, and weaves their everyday activities and their beliefs into a single cloth of religious devotion.

No matter how sincerely a person may believe, Islam regards it as pointless to live life without putting that faith into action and practice.

Carrying out the Five Pillars demonstrates that the Muslim is putting their faith first, and not just trying to fit it in around their secular lives.

Subdivisions within Islam

Sufism

Sufism, or Tasawwuf as it is known in the Muslim world, is loosely a form of Islamic mysticism. Non-Muslims often mistake Sufism as a sect of Islam. Sufism is more accurately described as an aspect or dimension of Islam. Sufi orders (Tariqas) can be found in Sunni, Shia and other Islamic groups.

Sunni and Shi'a

Sunni and Shi'a appear regularly in stories about the Muslim world but few people know what they really mean. Religion permeates every aspect of life in Muslim countries and understanding Sunni and Shi'a beliefs is important in understanding the modern Muslim world.

They both agree on the fundamentals of Islam and share the same Holy Book (The Qur'an), but there are differences mostly derived from their different historical experiences, political and social developments, as well as ethnic composition.

These differences originate from the question of who would succeed the Prophet Muhammad as leader of the emerging Muslim community after his death.

Jainism

Jainism is an ancient religion from India that teaches that the way to liberation and bliss is to live lives of harmlessness and renunciation. The essence of Jainism is concern for the welfare of every being in the universe and for the health of the universe itself.

Jains believe that animals and plants, as well as human beings, contain living souls. Each of these souls is considered of equal value and should be treated with respect and compassion.

Jains are strict vegetarians and live in a way that minimises their use of the world's resources. Jains believe in reincarnation and seek to attain ultimate liberation - which means escaping the continuous cycle of birth, death and rebirth so that the immortal soul lives for ever in a state of bliss.

Liberation is achieved by eliminating all karma from the soul.

Key facts

- Jainism is a religion of self-help.

- There are no gods or spiritual beings that will help human beings.

- The three guiding principles of Jainism, the 'three jewels', are right belief, right knowledge and right conduct.

- The supreme principle of Jain living is non-violence (ahimsa).

- This is one of the 5 mahavratas (the 5 great vows). The other mahavratas are non-attachment to possessions, not lying, not stealing, and sexual restraint (with celibacy as the ideal).

- Mahavira is regarded as the man who gave Jainism its present-day form.

- The texts containing the teachings of Mahavira are called the Agamas.

- Jains are divided into two major sects; the Digambara (meaning "sky clad") sect and the Svetambara (meaning "white clad") sect.

- Jainism has no priests. Its professional religious people are monks and nuns, who lead strict and ascetic lives.

Most Jains live in India, and according to the 2001 Census of India there are around 4.2 million living there. However, the Oxford Handbook of Global Religions, published in 2006, suggests that census figures may provide lower than the true number of followers as many Jains identify themselves as Hindu. The Handbook also states that there are around 25,000 Jains in Britain.

Daily spiritual practices

Jains try to carry out certain spiritual acts every day. These are:

- prayer

- honouring the tirthankaras

- paying respect to monks

- repenting for sins

- self-control through sitting meditation for 48 minutes

- going without something pleasurable

Spiritual routines & Worship

What follows is an outline of the spiritual routine of a particularly observant lay Jain - most Jains won't carry out all of this, although they will try to include as much as possible.

Morning prayers - before dawn

1) Panca Namaskara Sutra:

   I bow to the enlightened souls

   I bow to the liberated souls

   I bow to religious leaders

   I bow to religious teachers

   I bow to all the monks in the world

2) Pratikramana, repentance for harm done during the night.

3) temple visit for worship and hearing teaching

4) care for others

5) greetings and donations to monks and nuns

6) care for people in need

7) prayer before lunch

8) eat last meal of day before darkness falls

9) temple visit for worship (these visits are often replaced by ceremonies in the home)

10) Pratikramana - repentance for harm done during the day

11) reading of scriptures

At some point in the day, lay Jains try to fit in a 48-minute period of self-study and static meditation.

Jain temples

There are some beautiful Jain temples in India, although the majority of Jain temples are much plainer structures.

Jain temples contain images of tirthankaras; either in seated meditation or standing. A seated image or images is usually the focus of a temple interior. Jains make offerings to the images as part of their worship.

Jain temples range from the immense and elaborate to the very plainest of worship rooms.

The two largest Jain sects decorate their temples in different ways.

Digambara Jain temples have tirthankara statues that are undecorated and unpainted.

Svetambara Jain temples the images are always decorated - with painted or glass eyes and sometimes ornaments of gold, silver, and jewels on the forehead. Further decoration is common.

Svetambara Jains decorate faith images richly for festivals using flowers, paints, and jewels, and make decorative offerings of flowers, leaves, sandalwood, saffron, camphor, gold or silver leaf, pearls, precious stones or costume jewellery.

These offerings are renewed daily as a gesture of devotion.

For Jains, like Buddhists, the gods and idols are not real in themselves, rather symbols of human attitudes, aspirations and fears, so that worship is really about one's own integration in oneself and with the world around. Purity, right living and service of others are hallmarks of their faith.

Jehovah's Witness

Jehovah's Witnesses are members of a Christian-based religious movement. The denomination was founded in the USA towards the end of the 19th century, under the leadership of Charles Taze Russell.

There are about 6.9 million active Witnesses in 235 countries in the world (2007), including 1 million in the USA and 130,000 in the UK.

Members of the movement are probably best known for their door-to-door evangelical work; witnessing from house to house, offering Bible literature and recruiting and converting people to the truth.

Although Christian-based, the group believes that the traditional Christian Churches have deviated from the true teachings of the Bible, and do not work in full harmony with God.

The traditional Christian Churches, for their part, do not regard the movement as a mainstream Christian denomination because it rejects the Christian doctrine of the Trinity, which it regards as both irrational and unbiblical.

Beliefs

Jehovah's Witnesses base their beliefs only on the text of the Bible and ignore "mere human speculations or religious creeds." They believe that the Bible is the Word of God and consider its 66 books to be divinely inspired and historically accurate.

Members reject the sinful values of the secular world and maintain a degree of separation from non-believers - they are "in the world" but not "of the world".

Witnesses do not celebrate Christmas or Easter because they believe that these festivals are based on (or massively contaminated by) pagan customs and religions. They point out that Jesus did not ask his followers to mark his birthday.

Worship

Witnesses believe that the point of their life is to live in the service of God. They are expected to live in accord with the beliefs and moral code of the movement.

They live in a tightly knit social structure which supports them in both their everyday lives and in fulfilling their religious mission.

Separation

Jehovah's Witnesses maintain a degree of separation from the world. They claim that they are in but not of the world.

Unlike the members of more extreme separatist movements, Witnesses both live and work among the secular community and send their children to secular schools.

Witnesses discourage participation in university education for its own sake.

Witnesses are less likely to aspire to higher education than their peers... They typically disapprove of the rat race that is rife in contemporary society, and view earthly aspirations as being of much less importance than spiritual concerns: it is far preferable to work for Jehovah's kingdom than for material gain.

They also refuse military service, voting in elections, and taking part in most religious festivals and secular celebrations like birthdays. In countries with compulsory national service most Witnesses will accept civilian service as an alternative to military service. Certain civic obligations, such as jury service, are seen as a matter for individual decision according to the dictates of conscience.

The time spent on missionary work to non-believers prevents Witnesses from becoming significantly separated from the rest of the community.

Missionary work

In 2005 Jehovah's Witnesses around the world spent over 1.2 billion hours on missionary work. All Witnesses who are physically capable of it engage in missionary work.

Much missionary work involves visiting door-to-door to discuss scripture with people they meet. A successful discussion will lead to return trips, and possibly to home Bible studies. The aim is to persuade a non-believer of the rightness of their cause so that they eventually become a Witness themselves.

Witnesses place little emphasis on sudden, dramatic conversion experiences. True conversion is a slow intellectual process which gradually convinces a non-believer that Witness beliefs are true and rational, and that they should commit themselves to a spiritually rewarding life that will bring eternal benefits.

Witnesses believe that missionary work should take priority over career, so many will choose lower-paid jobs with limited hours so as to have more time to devote to their faith.

Discipline and disfellowshipping

Jehovah's Witnesses are expected to accept the movement's core beliefs and practices. If they act in a way that is incompatible with such beliefs and practices, they may be disciplined. But for an allegation to be proved against someone, that person must confess or, in line with the Bible's teaching, there must be two witnesses.

Serious transgressions are dealt with by quasi-judicial local hearings. When someone either confesses to or is accused of a sin or spiritual transgression, he or she is questioned by elders.

If they are found guilty, they can be punished by spiritual restrictions, public reproofs or expulsion from the congregation, which is called 'disfellowshipping'.

Disfellowshipping is the Witnesses' highest form of discipline. It is reserved for deliberate apostasy or unrepentantly practising serious sins such as drunkenness, stealing or adultery. Disfellowshipped persons can be reinstated into the congregation after demonstrating that they are repentant.

Elders disfellowship 50,000 to 60,000 Witnesses around the world every year. Each year, however, 30,000 to 40,000 are reinstated having "come back to their spiritual senses".

Members of the movement were originally called Bible Students. The name Jehovah's Witnesses was adopted in 1931. The church is strongly millennial and believes that humanity is now in the 'last days' and that the final battle between good and evil will happen soon.

Judaism

Judaism is the original of the three Abrahamic faiths, which also includes Christianity and Islam.

According to information published by The Jewish People Policy Planning Institute, there were around 13.1 million Jewish people in the world in 2007, most residing in the USA and Israel. According to the 2001 census 267,000 people in the UK said that their religious identity was Jewish, about 0.5% of the population.

Key facts

- Judaism originated in the Middle East over 3500 years ago

- Judaism was founded by Moses, although Jews trace their history back to Abraham.

- Jews believe that there is only one God with whom they have a covenant.

- In exchange for all the good that God has done for the Jewish people, Jewish people keep God's laws and try to bring holiness into every aspect of their lives.

- Judaism has a rich history of religious text, but the central and most important religious document is the Torah.

- Jewish traditional or oral law, the interpretation of the laws of the Torah, is called halakhah.

- Spiritual leaders are called Rabbis.

- Jews worship in Synagogues.

- 6 million Jews were murdered in the Holocaust in an attempt to wipe out Judaism.

There are many people who identify themselves as Jewish without necessarily believing in, or observing, any Jewish law.

Worship and prayers

Jews believe that prayer builds the relationship between God and human beings.

Jews, like other people of faith, pray in many different ways.

- They pray so that their hearts can reach out to God

- They pray to express and exercise their beliefs

- They pray to share in the life of a worshipping community

- They pray to obey God's commandments

Jews are supposed to pray three times a day; morning, afternoon, and evening. The Jewish prayer book (called a siddur) has special services set down for this.

There are three different sorts of prayer, and Jewish people use all of them. These are prayers of thanksgiving, prayers of praise, and prayers that ask for things

The formal prayer in the synagogue provides a weekly (if not daily) revision class in the fundamentals of Jewish belief

Public prayer

Much of Jewish prayer consists of reciting the written services aloud in synagogue.

Praying in public affirms that a person is a member of a community, and when they do so, an individual puts themselves into the context of other Jews, and to some extent puts their own particular situation aside to put the community first.

It's also an act of togetherness with Jewish people who are doing the same all around the world.

The prayer book

The Jewish prayer book is drawn from the writings of the Jewish people across the ages. It contains the wisdom of great thinkers, and some of the most beautiful Hebrew poetry.

Subdivisions and denominations

- Conservative Judaism

- Humanistic Judaism

- Liberal Judaism

- Modern Orthodoxy

- Orthodox Judaism

- Reconstructionist Judaism

- Reform Judaism

Latter Day Saints

The Church of Jesus Christ of Latter-day Saints was founded in 19th century America and has 13.5 million members world-wide (LDS 2008 Statistical Report).

'Mormonism' has been present in the UK since 1837 and has 190,000 members (LDS 2008 figures).

Key Facts

- The church is called The Church of Jesus Christ of Latter-day Saints, or The Church of Jesus Christ.

- Mormons believe their church is a restoration of the Church as conceived by Jesus and that the other Christian churches have gone astray.

- The church was founded by Joseph Smith (1805 - 1844).

- It was then developed by Brigham Young who migrated with the new Mormons to Salt Lake City in 1847.

- Mormons believe that God has a physical body, is married, and can have children.

- They also believe that humans can become gods in the afterlife.

- Mormons are strongly focused on traditional family life and values.

- They oppose abortion, homosexuality, unmarried sexual acts, pornography, gambling, tobacco, consuming alcohol, tea, coffee, and the use of drugs.

- One of the more common misconceptions is that The Church of Jesus Christ of Latter-day Saints advocates polygamy. However, this was discontinued over a century ago and the Church excommunicates anyone who practices it.

Worship

Communal worship in The Church of Jesus Christ of Latter-day Saints is rather informal and doesn't involve ceremonials or priests. It takes place in a simple Chapel, which doesn't have religious statues or pictures.

The service is organised and conducted by unpaid lay members of the congregation, as the Church does not have clergy. Most Mormon families will spend about three hours with their local community each Sunday. Some of this time is taken with adult learning or Sunday School, and with various meetings.

The Sacrament Meeting

The Sacrament Meeting lasts 70 minutes and involves the whole community together. It's very much a family affair, so there are usually lots of children present.

During the service the members receive a sacramental communion of bread and water, during which they remember the Last Supper, the Atonement of Jesus Christ, and their own baptismal promises to serve the Lord and keep his commandments. The sacrament is distributed by Deacons.

The service is led by the bishop, and his two counsellors. The bishop is the ecclesiastical leader of the local Church, and is a lay minister.

The service begins with hymns followed by prayers.

There will be a number of short talks or sermons given by members of the congregation chosen by the bishop. These talks range from quite formal doctrinal lectures, to more informal chats about the application of faith to family life. Talks can be given by church members right across the age range.

Mormons always make a point of dressing smartly and respectfully for services.

Non-Mormons are welcome to visit Mormon services.

Paganism

Paganism describes a group of contemporary religions based on a reverence for nature. These faiths draw on the traditional religions of indigenous peoples throughout the world.

Paganism encompasses a diverse community; Wiccans, Druids, Shamans, Sacred Ecologists, Odinists, Goddess Community and Heathens all make up parts of the Pagan community.

Some groups concentrate on specific traditions or practices such as ecology, witchcraft, Celtic traditions or certain gods.

Most Pagans share an ecological vision that comes from the Pagan belief in the organic vitality and spirituality of the natural world.

Pagans are not sexual deviants, do not worship the devil, are not evil, do not practice 'black magic' and their practices do not involve harming people or animals.

The Pagan Federation of Great Britain have no precise figures but estimate that the number of Pagans in the British Isles is between 50,000 and 200,000 (2002).

Key beliefs

Nature

The recognition of the divine in nature is at the heart of Pagan belief. Pagans are deeply aware of the natural world and see the power of the divine in the ongoing cycle of life and death. Most Pagans are eco-friendly, seeking to live in a way that minimises harm to the natural environment.

Concepts of the divine

Pagans worship the divine in many different forms, through feminine as well as masculine imagery and also as without gender. The most important and widely recognised of these are the God and Goddess (or pantheons of God and Goddesses) whose annual cycle of procreation, giving birth and dying defines the Pagan year. Paganism strongly emphasises equality of the sexes. Women play a prominent role in the modern Pagan movement, and Goddess worship features in most Pagan ceremonies.

Pagan theology

Paganism is not based on doctrine or liturgy. Many pagans believe 'if it harms none, do what you will'. Following this code, Pagan theology is based primarily on experience, with the aim of Pagan ritual being to make contact with the divine in the world that surrounds them.

As Paganism is a very diverse religion with many distinct though related traditions, the forms of Pagan worship vary widely. It may be collective or solitary. It may consist of informal prayer or meditation, or of formal, structured rituals through which the participants affirm their deep spiritual connection with nature, honour their Gods and Goddesses, and celebrate the seasonal festivals of the turning year and the rites of passage of human life.

Worship and practice

As Pagans have no public buildings specifically set aside for worship, and most believe that religious ceremonies are best conducted out of doors, rituals often take place in woods or caves, on hilltops, or along the seashore. To Pagans the finest places of worship are those not built by human hands - as well as at stone circles, in parks, and private homes and gardens. Women and men almost always worship together, and Paganism generally emphasises equality of the sexes. In certain paths, however, women may take the leading role as representative of the pre-eminence of the female principle.

Ceremonies usually begin with the marking out of a ritual circle, a symbol of sacred space which has neither beginning nor end, and within which all stand as equals. At the quarter-points, the four directions and the corresponding elements of Earth, Air, Fire and Water will be acknowledged and bid welcome.

Pagans do not believe that they are set above, or apart from, the rest of nature. They understand divinity to be immanent, woven through every aspect of the living earth. Thus, Pagan worship is mainly concerned with connection to, and the honouring of, immanent divinity.

Rastafari

Rastafari is a young, Africa-centred religion which developed in Jamaica in the 1930s, following the coronation of Haile Selassie I as King of Ethiopia in 1930.

Rastafarians believe Haile Selassie is God and that he will return to Africa members of the community who are living in exile as the result of colonisation and the slave trade.

Rastafari theology developed from the ideas of Marcus Garvey, a political activist who wanted to improve the status of the black community.

There are approximately one million world-wide adherents of Rastafari as a faith. The 2001 census found 5,000 Rastafarians living in England and Wales.

Followers of Rastafari are known by a variety of names: Rastafarians, Rastas, Sufferers, Locksmen, Dreads or Dreadlocks.

It spread globally following the success of Bob Marley and

his music in the 1970s. Rastafarians believe that Black people are the chosen people of God, but that through colonisation and the slave trade their role has been suppressed.

The movement's greatest concerns are the repatriation of former Black slave families to their homeland, Africa, and the reinstatement of black people's position in society

It is an exocentric religion - as Haile Selassie, whom adherents consider as God, is outside the religion.

Rastafari religious ceremonies consist of chanting, drumming and meditating in order to reach a state of heightened spirituality, using elements of the older Afrikaans faiths.

Rastafarian religious practice includes the ritual inhalation of marijuana, to increase their spiritual awareness, dietary laws and abstain from alcohol. They follow a number of Old Testament Laws.

Key facts

- There is a separate code of religious practice for women in Rastafari.

- Rastafarians believe reincarnation follows death and that life is eternal.

- Rastafarians are forbidden to cut their hair; instead, they grow it and twist it into dreadlocks.

- Rastafarians eat clean and natural produce, such as fruit and vegetables.

- Rastafarians try to refrain from the consumption of meat, especially pork.

- Rastafarians are opposed to abortion and contraception.

Rastafarian colours

The Rastafarian colours are red, green and gold. Sometimes black is added.

These colours are chosen because:

- Red signifies the blood of those killed for the cause of the black community, throughout Jamaican history

- Green represents Jamaica's vegetation and hope for the eradication of suppression

- Gold symbolises the wealth of Ethiopia

- Black signifies the colour of the Africans who initiated Rastafari

Worship

Rastafari doesn't have a specific religious building that is set aside for worship. Rastafarians usually meet weekly, either in a believer's home or in a community centre.

The meetings are referred to as Reasoning sessions. They provide a time for chants, prayers and singing, and for communal issues to be discussed. Marijuana may be smoked to produce heightened spiritual states.

The music used at these meetings is known as Nyabingi, and so when meetings are mostly musical they are often referred to as Nyabingi meetings. Meetings may also include large feasts.

Marijuana

Regarded as a herb of religious significance. It is used in Rastafari reasoning sessions, which are communal meetings involving meditation.

Rastafarians first began using Marijuana in reaction to the treatment of blacks in society. It became a reactionary device to enable freedom from the establishment. (Leonard Barrett, The Rastafarians, The Dreadlocks of Jamaica p. 129)

Marijuana is used by Rastafarians to heighten feelings of community and to produce visions of a religious and calming nature.

Rastafarians are unlikely to refer to the substance as marijuana; they usually describe it as the wisdom weed or the holy herb.

The latter name is used because Rastafarians believe that marijuana use is sacred. The use of marijuana is a highly ritualised act, and before it is used a prayer is uttered by all:

The marijuana is rolled into a cigarette or placed into a chillum pipe. When smoked it is inhaled deeply, then held, as the devotee enters into a trance-like state.

Dreadlocks

Rastafarians can often be recognised from the way they style their hair. Rastafarians grow their hair long, before coiling it into dreadlocks. The wearing of hair in dreadlocks by Rastafarians is believed to be spiritual.

Food laws

Rastafarians eat strictly I-tal which means natural and clean

- Early Rastafarians are unlikely to eat meat, scavengers or shellfish

- Rastafarians do not eat pork

- Rastafarians regularly eat fish, but will not eat fish more than twelve inches long

- Rastafarians eat copious amounts of vegetables, as they are of the earth, and therefore good

- Food is prepared without salt, and coconut oil is the most likely form of oil to be utilised

- Rastafarians do not drink alcohol

- They do not drink milk or coffee, but will drink anything herbal, grown from natural roots, e.g. herbal tea

- Rastafarians consume plentiful amounts of fruit and fruit juice

Santeria

Santeria (Way of the Saints) is an Afro-Caribbean religion based on Yoruba beliefs and traditions, with some Roman Catholic elements added. The religion is also known as La Regla Lucumi and the Rule of Osha.

Santeria is a syncretic religion that grew out of the slave trade in Cuba. The religion focuses on building relationships between human beings and powerful, but mortal, spirits, called Orishas. An Orisha is a manifestation of Olodumare (God).

Followers believe that these spirits will give them help in life, if they carry out the appropriate rituals, and enable them to achieve the destiny that God planned for them before they were born.

This is very much a mutual relationship as the Orishas need to be worshipped by human beings if they are to continue to exist. Orishas can be perceived in the physical universe by initiates, and the whole community can share in their presence when they possess a priest during some rituals.

Influence of Catholicism

- The Roman Catholic element in Santeria is most obvious in the way Orishas are associated with Catholic Saints such as:

- Saint Barbara [Shangó], who embodies justice and strength, and is associated with lightning and fire

- Our Lady of Charity [Ochún] - the Yoruba goddess of the river, associated with water, yellow, sweets, money, and love

- Saint Lazarus [Babalú-Ayé] - who is associated with the sick

- Followers of Santeria are often (nominal) Roman Catholics as well. Catholic symbols are sometimes used in Santeria rituals.

Holy Books

Santeria has no scriptures and is passed on by word-of-mouth.

Priesthood

Santeria has a priesthood that includes both men and women. Priesthood involves training and initiation.

The priest may be a babalorisha (Father in the Spirit) or iyalorisha (Mother or Wife in the Spirit). The Spanish words for these priests are santero or santera.

Priesthood is not a full-time paid job, and is often combined with ordinary work.

A priest has 'made the saint', which means that they have been 'reborn in the spirit' and made a commitment to serve a particular Orisha.

Priests have special powers because they have been 'entered' by an Orisha. These powers are thought to allow them to predict the future.

Divination mediates between earth (aiye) and heaven (orun). It proffers counsel and guidance to believers at all critical junctures and transitional experiences of the life cycle.

Divination can be done by casting palm nuts, interpreting the fall of shells, or using a divided coconut.

Santeria also includes the Yoruba divination system called Ifa, which can only be performed by a senior male priest called a babalawo. This ritual involves throwing an ekwele, a chain of 8 shaped pieces. The way in which these pieces fall is used to provide guidance.

Healthcare

Santeria priests have a great knowledge of traditional medicine and herbalism, and often play an important role in the health of their community.

Their healthcare draws on Catholicism as well as African tradition; holy water is an ingredient in many Santeria medicinal formulas.

Santeria healthcare is often combined with conventional medicine.

Shinto

The essence of Shinto is the Japanese devotion to invisible spiritual beings and powers called kami, to shrines, and to various rituals. Shinto is not a way of explaining the world. What matters are rituals that enable human beings to communicate with kami.

Kami are not God or gods. They are spirits that are concerned with human beings - they appreciate our interest in them and want us to be happy - and if they are treated properly, they will intervene in our lives to bring benefits like health, business success, and good exam results.

Shinto is a very local religion, in which devotees are likely to be concerned with their local shrine rather than the religion as a whole. Many Japanese will have a tiny shrine-altar in their homes.

However, it is also an unofficial national religion with shrines that draw visitors from across the country. Because ritual rather than belief is at the heart of Shinto, Japanese people don't usually think of Shinto specifically as a religion - it's simply an aspect of Japanese life. This has enabled Shinto to coexist happily with Buddhism for centuries.

Key facts

- The name Shinto comes from Chinese characters for Shen ('divine being'), and Tao ('way') and means 'Way of the Spirits'.

- Shrine visiting and taking part in festivals play a great part in binding local communities together.

- Shrine visiting at New Year is the most popular shared national event in Japan.

- Because Shinto is focussed on the land of Japan it is clearly an ethnic religion. Therefore, Shinto is little interested in missionary work, and rarely practised outside its country of origin.

- Shinto sees human beings as basically good and has no concept of original sin, or of humanity as 'fallen'.

- Everything, including the spiritual, is experienced as part of this world. Shinto has no place for any transcendental other world.

- Shinto has no canonical scriptures.

- Shinto teaches important ethical principles but has no commandments.

- Shinto has no founder.

- Shinto has no God.

- Shinto does not require adherents to follow it as their only religion.

Shinto worship

Shinto worship is highly ritualised, and follows strict conventions of protocol, order and control. It can take place in the home or in shrines. Although all Shinto worship and ritual takes place within the patterns set when the faith was centralised in the 19th century, there is much local diversity.

The spirit of Shinto worship

In keeping with Shinto values, Shinto ritual should be carried out in a spirit of sincerity, cheerfulness and purity.

Shinto worship and the senses

Shinto ritual is intended to satisfy the senses as well as the minds of those taking part, so the way in which it is carried out is of huge importance. Shinto ceremonies have strong aesthetic elements - the setting and props, the sounds, the dress of the priests, and the language and speech are all intended to please the kami to whom the worship is offered.

Private and public worship

Although Shinto worship features public and shared rituals at local shrines, it can also be a private and individual event, in which a person at a shrine (or in their home) prays to particular kami either to obtain something, or to thank the kami for something good that has happened.

Worship at home

Many Japanese homes contain a place set aside as a shrine, called a *kami-dana* (kami shelf), where they may make offerings of flowers or food, and say prayers.

The kami-dana is a shelf that contains a tiny replica of the sanctuary of a shrine, and may also include amulets bought to ensure good luck (or absorb bad luck). A mirror in the centre connects the shelf to the kami.

If a family has bought a religious object at a shrine they will lay this on the kami-dana, thus linking home to shrine.

Worship at a shrine

There is no special day of the week for worship in Shinto - people visit shrines for festivals, for personal spiritual reasons, or to put a particular request to the kami (this might be for good luck in an exam, or protection of a family member, and so on).

Worship takes place in shrines built with great understanding of the natural world. The contrast between the human ritual and the natural world underlines the way in which Shinto constructs and reflects human empathy for the universe.

The journey that the worshipper makes through the shrine to the sanctuary where the ritual takes place forms part of the worship, and helps the worshipper to move spiritually from the everyday world to a place of holiness and purity.

The aesthetics (or to put it over simply, the 'look') of the shrine contribute substantially to the worship, in the way that the setting of a theatre play contributes significantly to the overall drama.

Although Shinto rituals appear very ancient, many are actually modern revivals, or even modern inventions.

Sikhism

There are 20 million Sikhs in the world, most of whom live in the Punjab province of India. The 2001 census recorded 336,000 Sikhs in the UK.

Sikhism was founded in the 16th century in the Punjab district of what is now India and Pakistan. It was founded by Guru Nanak and is based on his teachings, and those of the 9 Sikh gurus who followed him.

The most important thing in Sikhism is the internal religious state of the individual.

Key Facts

- Sikhism is a monotheistic religion

- Sikhism stresses the importance of doing good actions rather than merely carrying out rituals

- Sikhs believe that the way to lead a good life is to:

- keep God in heart and mind at all times

- live honestly and work hard

- treat everyone equally

- be generous to the less fortunate

- serve others

- The Sikh place of worship is called a Gurdwara

- The Sikh scripture is the Guru Granth Sahib, a book that Sikhs consider a living Guru

The tenth Sikh Guru decreed that after his death the spiritual guide of the Sikhs would be the teachings contained in that book, so the Guru Granth Sahib now has the status of a Guru, and Sikhs show it the respect they would give to a human Guru.

Guru Gobind Singh decreed that where Sikhs could not find answers in the Guru Granth Sahib, they should decide issues as a community, based on the principles of their scripture.

Sikh worship

Sikhs worship God and only God. Unlike members of many other religions they worship God in his true abstract form, and don't use images or statues to help them.

Sikh worship can be public or private.

Private worship

Sikhs can pray at any time and any place. Sikh aims to get up early, bathe, and then start the day by meditating on God.

There are set prayers that a Sikh should recite in the morning and evening, and before going to sleep.

Although the Sikh God is beyond description Sikhs feel able to pray to God as a person and a friend who cares for them. Sikhs regard prayer as a way of spending time in company with God.

Public worship

Although Sikhs can worship on their own, they see congregational worship as having its own special merits.

Sikhs believe that God is visible in the Sikh congregation or Sangat, and that God is pleased by the act of serving the Sangat.

Sikh public worship can be led by any Sikh, male or female, who is competent to do so.

Congregational Sikh worship takes place in a Gurdwara.

Gurdwara

The literal meaning of the Punjabi word Gurdwara is 'the residence of the Guru', or 'the door that leads to the Guru'.

In a Gurdwara, the Guru is not a person but the book of Sikh scriptures called the Guru Granth Sahib. It is the presence of the Guru Granth Sahib that gives the Gurdwara its religious status, so any building containing the book is a Gurdwara.

Although a Gurdwara may be called the residence of the Guru (meaning the residence of God), Sikhs believe that God is present everywhere.

Before the time of Guru Arjan Dev, the place of Sikh religious activities was known as a Dharamsala, which means place of faith.

Inside a Gurdwara

There are no idols, statues, or religious pictures in a Gurdwara, because Sikhs worship only God, and they regard God as having no physical form. Nor are there candles, incense, or bells, or any other ritualistic devices.

The focus of attention, and the only object of reverence in the main hall (or Darbar Sahib) is the book of Sikh scripture, the Guru Granth Sahib, which is treated with the respect that would be given to a human Guru.

The Guru Granth Sahib is kept in a room of its own during the night and carried in procession to the main hall at the start of the day's worship.

The book is placed on a raised platform (Takht or Manji Sahib, meaning "throne") under a canopy (Chanani or Palki), and covered with an expensive cloth when not being read.

During a service a person with a whisk or fan called a Chaur waves it over the Guru Granth Sahib.

Although Sikhs show reverence to the Guru Granth Sahib, their reverence is to its spiritual content (shabad) not the book itself. The book is just the visible manifestation of the shabad.

The four doors

There are four doors into a Gurdwara, known as the Door of Peace, the Door of Livelihood, the Door of Learning and the Door of Grace.

These doors are a symbol that people from all four points of the compass are welcome, and that members of all four castes are equally welcome.

There's always a light on in a Gurdwara, to show that the Guru's Light is always visible and is accessible to everyone at any time.

Flying the flag

Gurdwaras fly the Sikh flag outside. The flag is orange/yellow and has the Sikh emblem in the middle.

The free food kitchen, or Langar

Sikh men serve food inside a Langar. Every Gurdwara has a Langar attached to it where food is served to anyone without charge. The term Langar is also used for the communal meal served at the Gurdwaras.

The food served in the Langar must be simple, so as to prevent wealthy congregations turning it into a feast that shows off their superiority.

Food Requirements

Although Sikhs are not required to be vegetarian, only vegetarian food is served in the Gurdwaras. This ensures that any visitor to the Gurdwara, whatever the dietary restrictions of their faith, can eat in the Langar.

The meal may include chapati, dal (pulses), vegetables and rice pudding. Fish and eggs are counted as meat and excluded.

Spiritualism

Spiritualists communicate with the spirits of people who have physically died. Such communication is thought to be beneficial to the dead and the living. Spiritualists are those who believe in a continued future existence, and that people who have passed on into the spirit-world can and do communicate with us.

Spirits are said to communicate through people with special skills, called mediums. In the 19th Century communication was said to have occurred at an event called a séance but in the 21st Century most communication is said to take place either in a public demonstration of mediumship at a Spiritualist church service or in a private sitting with a medium. Communication can be verbal, such as messages; or physical manifestations, such as tapping.

Spiritualism is different from the world's major and minor religions (Christianity, Judaism, Islam etc) because it's recent, it doesn't have a global presence, it doesn't have a body of theology. However, it is a new religious movement with rituals, doctrinal components, a belief in a transcendent realm, and it has an experiential dimension, elements that many other religions also have.

Spiritualism sees itself as entirely rational, with no element of the supernatural. For Spiritualists, this is what distinguishes their beliefs from the concept of life after death found in many other faiths.

It is said to be the eighth largest religion in Britain and has a network of groups across the country. The total of SNU-affiliated and associated bodies in the UK is 360, broken down into 348 affiliated bodies and 12 associated bodies.

Those who follow it are united in believing that communication with spirits is possible; but beyond this central idea Modern Spiritualism can include a very wide range of beliefs and world-views.

Key ideas

Spiritualists generally believe the following:

- Souls survive bodily death and live in a spirit world - Spiritualists say that every human soul survives the death of the body and enters a spirit-world that surrounds and interpenetrates the material world.

- These souls can communicate with the material world - Spiritualists say that communication is possible between the material world and the spirit-world under the right conditions - usually through a medium.

- Spirit beings are little changed from their earlier selves - Spiritualists say that those in the spirit-world are much the same as they were in the material world, although without any physical deficiencies.

- Spirit beings are interested in people in the material world - Spiritualists say that those in the spirit world are aware of and interested in the lives of those they have temporarily left behind in the material world.

Seven Principles

The core philosophy of Spiritualism is described in The Seven Principles.

1) The Fatherhood of God

2) The Brotherhood of Man

3) The Communion of Spirits and the Ministry of Angels

4) The continuous existence of the human soul

5) Personal responsibility

6) Compensation and retribution hereafter for all the good and evil deeds done on earth

7) Eternal progress open to every human soul

Spiritualists sometimes refer to Spiritualism as a Religion, a Philosophy and a Science. They regard their religion as based on universal truths:

Many Spiritualists believe that Christianity and Spiritualism are compatible, but many Christians would disagree.

Daoism

Daoism is an ancient tradition of philosophy and religious belief that is deeply rooted in Chinese customs and worldview. Taoism is also referred to as Daoism, which is a more accurate way of representing in English the sound of the Chinese word.

Daoism is about the Dao. This is usually translated as the Way. The Dao is the ultimate creative principle of the universe. All things are unified and connected in the Dao.

Daoism originated in China 2000 years ago

It is a religion of unity and opposites; Yin and Yang. The principle of Yin Yang sees the world as filled with complementary forces - action and non-action, light and dark, hot and cold, and so on.

The Dao is not God and is not worshipped. Daoism includes many deities, that are worshipped in Daoist temples, they are part of the universe and depend, like everything, on the Dao

Daoism promotes:

- achieving harmony or union with nature

- the pursuit of spiritual immortality

- being 'virtuous' (but not ostentatiously so)

- self-development

Taoist practices include:

- meditation

- feng shui

- fortune telling

- reading and chanting of scriptures

Before the Communist revolution fifty years ago, Daoism was one of the strongest religions in China. After a campaign to destroy non-Communist religion, however, the numbers significantly reduced, and it has become difficult to assess the statistical popularity of Daoism in the world. Many Daoists and monks have converted to Buddhism in recent centuries, acknowledging the shared values, history and philosophy of both religions.

The 2001 census recorded 3,500 Taoists in England and Wales.

Key Worship Practices

- Alchemy

- Body and spirit

- Physical practices

- Recitation

- Sexual energy

- ChaDao (Tea)

- Talismans

At the heart of Daoist ritual is the concept of bringing order and harmony to many layers of the cosmos: the cosmos as a whole (the world of nature), the world or human society, and the inner world of human individuals.

Daoist rituals involve purification, meditation and offerings to deities. The details of Daoist rituals are often highly complex and technical and therefore left to the priests, with the congregation playing little part.

The rituals involve the priest (and assistants) in chanting and playing instruments (particularly wind and percussion), and also dancing.

One major Daoist ritual is the chiao (jiao), a rite of cosmic renewal, which is itself made up of several rituals.

A shortened version of the chiao is a ritual in which each household in a village brings an offering for the local deities. In the ceremony a Daoist priest dedicates the offerings in the names of the families, performs a ritual to restore order to the universe, and asks the gods to bring peace and prosperity to the village.

Temple rituals

Temple rituals can be used to regulate ch'i and balance the flow of yin and yang both for individuals and the wider community.

Other rituals involve prayers to various Daoist deities, meditations on talismans, and reciting and chanting prayers and texts.

Unitarianism

Unitarianism is an open-minded and individualistic approach to religion that gives scope for a very wide range of beliefs and doubts.

Religious freedom for each individual is at the heart of Unitarianism. Everyone is free to search for meaning in life in a responsible way and to reach their own conclusions.

There are about 7,000 Unitarians in Great Britain and Ireland, and about 150 Unitarian ministers. There are about 800,000 Unitarians worldwide.

In line with their approach to religious truth, Unitarians see diversity and pluralism as valuable rather than threatening. They want religion to be broad, inclusive, and tolerant. Unitarianism can therefore include people who are Christian, Jewish, Buddhist, Pagan and Atheist.

Key notes

- Unitarianism has no standard set of beliefs

- Unitarians believe that religious truth is not necessarily or primarily laid down either in scriptures, by a holy person or by a religious institution

- no individual or group in Unitarianism makes an exclusive claim to the truth

- within certain core values each Unitarian can believe what they feel is right

- Unitarians are so called because they insist on the oneness of God and because they affirm the essential unity of humankind and of creation

- Unitarians believe religion should make a difference to the world, so they are often active in social justice and community work

- Unitarianism grew out of the Protestant Reformation of the 16th century CE and started in Poland and Transylvania in the 1560s

- Unitarians have adopted the Flaming Chalice as the symbol of their faith

- The Unitarians were the first church in Britain to

accept women as ministers, in 1904

- Unitarians welcome gays and lesbians in their ministry and support equal rights for gay people within the Church and in society at large

Worship

Unitarians are unconvinced by ideas of God as an all-powerful Being who demands praise and obedience in return for the promise of individual salvation.

Equally, the focus of the service may be simply the celebration of life itself, providing opportunities for an expression of the human sense of wonder.

Each congregation can devise its own form of service, so there is a wide variety. In general, Unitarian services lack liturgy and ritual, but do contain readings from many sources, sermons, prayers, silences, and hymns and songs.

Unitarian worship will tend to use gender-inclusive language, as well as language and concepts drawn from a wide range of religious and philosophical traditions.

Won Buddhism

The name "Won Buddhism" comes from the Korean words 원/圓 won ("circle") and 불교/佛敎 bulgyo ("Buddhism"), literally meaning "Round Buddhism" or interpreted as "Consummate Buddhism." It is a different faith system to 'Buddhism' despite the similarity of the name.

By "consummate," Won Buddhists mean that they incorporate several different schools of traditional Buddhist thought into their doctrine; that is, where some schools focus only on practicing meditation (samādhi), some schools devote themselves fully to studying scriptures (prajñā), and still others practice only their school's precepts (śīla), Won Buddhism believes in incorporating all three into daily practice.

Zoroastrianism

Zoroastrianism is one of the world's oldest monotheistic religions. It was founded by the Prophet Zoroaster (or Zarathustra) in ancient Iran approximately 3500 years ago.

For 1000 years Zoroastrianism was one of the most powerful religions in the world. It was the official religion of Persia (Iran) from 600 BCE to 650 CE. It is now one of the world's smallest religions. In 2016 the New York Times reported that there were probably less than 190,000 followers worldwide at that time.

Zoroastrians believe there is one God called Ahura Mazda (Wise Lord) and He created the world.

Zoroastrians are not fire-worshippers, as some Westerners wrongly believe. Zoroastrians believe that the elements are pure and that fire represents God's light or wisdom.

Key notes

- Ahura Mazda revealed the truth through the Prophet, Zoroaster.

- Zoroastrians traditionally pray several times a day.

- Zoroastrians worship communally in a Fire Temple or Agiary.

- The Zoroastrian book of Holy Scriptures is called The Avesta.

- The Avesta can be roughly split into two main sections:

- The Avesta is the oldest and core part of the scriptures, which contains the Gathas. The Gathas are seventeen hymns thought to be composed by Zoroaster himself.

- The Younger Avesta - commentaries to the older Avestan written in later years. It also contains myths, stories and details of ritual observances.

Zoroastrians are roughly split into two groups:

The Iranians and the The Parsis

Worship

Zoroaster placed less emphasis on ritual worship, instead focusing on the central ethics of 'Good Words, Good Thoughts and Good Deeds'.

Zoroastrian worship is not prescriptive. Its followers can choose whether they wish to pray and how.

Communal worship is usually centred around seasonal festivals (of which the Zoroastrians have many), but there are other opportunities for worshipers to gather, such as the Navjote, the initiation ceremony where a child is accepted into the Zoroastrian fellowship.

Prayers

Zoroastrians traditionally pray several times a day. Some wear a kusti, which is a cord knotted three times, to remind them of the maxim, 'Good Words, Good Thoughts, Good Deeds'. They wrap the kusti around the outside of a sudreh, a long, clean, white cotton shirt. They may engage in a purification ritual, such as the washing of the hands, then untie and then retie it while reciting prayers.

Prayers are primarily invocational, calling upon and celebrating Ahura Mazda and his good essence that runs through all things. Prayers are said facing the sun, fire or other source of light representing Ahura Mazda's divine light and energy.

Purification is strongly emphasised in Zoroastrian rituals. Zoroastrians focus on keeping their minds, bodies and environments pure in the quest to defeat evil (Angra Mainyu). Fire is seen as the supreme symbol of purity, and sacred fires are maintained in Fire Temples (Agiaries). These fires represent the light of God (Ahura Mazda) as well as the illuminated mind, and are never extinguished. No Zoroastrian ritual or ceremony is performed without the presence of a sacred fire.

Community Characteristics
& Communications

An introductory guide to terminology, respectful ways to establish communications or pass information. Together with expanded discussions on community relevant subjects.

This section is intended to give you a guide to using terminology, understand the characteristics and sensitivities of each area of inclusion and use as a reference tool for further discussion, investigation or communication.

Age

Age is unlike other equality issues. It affects us all. We are all young at some time in our lives and we all expect to get old.

Older People

Being old is still equated far too often with undesirable or negative social attributes, including dependency, rigidity of thought and the inability to learn new things. Factually, such views are incorrect. The vast majority of today's older people are active, fit and independent. The personality traits which are frequently used to describe them in disparaging terms are to be found in some people at all ages and stages of life. They have nothing to do with the process of ageing itself.

Language is a powerful method of structuring attitudes about old age. In this area our language is highly expressive and almost invariably derogatory, pitying or condescending. Words and phrases in common usage, such as 'mutton dressed as lamb', 'crinklies', 'dirty old man', 'old fogey', 'old codger', 'old dear' and 'old folk' all conjure up images which leave little doubt about attitudes to old age. Careful choice of language will help to shape the perspective presented.

It is advisable to avoid the term 'the elderly' as this is now regarded by some as depersonalising and distancing and has connotations of dependency and frailty. Other terms, such as 'pensioners' and 'senior citizens', are accepted by some and rejected by others. 'Older People' is generally accepted by all.

Images should be avoided which portray older people as clumsy, frail, pathetic and needing to be helped, while younger members of the family are happily enjoying an exciting life. Similarly, the link that is assumed between beauty and youth implies a link between old age and ugliness this is detrimental to older people. The best images portray older people as rounded individuals, participating in society.

Young People

For younger people, language and image can easily reinforce stereotypes. The image of young people as carefree, without any pressures or worries or without adequate life experience to make informed decisions can be entirely misleading.

Some young people are carers, have worked from an early age, have suffered hardship and have had major successes in their lives. Expectations of younger people can also be based on stereotypes – for example, not all younger people are computer experts or intuitive to the latest technologies.

It is also important to understand young people wish to be treated with respect, dignity and intelligence as would an adult. To this end avoid using condescending language styles or tone, or images which show young people being 'lead' by adult.

It is important to realise that Older People and Young People come from all areas of the community, may or may not have a faith and may or may not be disabled.

Ethnicity, cultural

& faith diversity

We live in a multicultural society, with a rich variety of traditions, cultures and values. However, we are all aware of racism: those beliefs and attitudes expressed in forms of behaviour and institutionalised practices, which serve to discriminate against or to marginalise people judged to be of another 'race'.

We are concerned here with unintentional racism, whereby the views, values and attitudes of the dominant (in the UK, white) group are exclusively presented. It can be hard for people to realise that this is in fact what is happening as it is often implicit rather than overt.

Teaching materials alone cannot redress inequalities in society, but they should not reinforce and perpetuate untrue assumptions and beliefs. The process of education should challenge such prejudices and ignorance. It can go further than that: it can become a means of increasing understanding, particularly the majority culture's knowledge of minority ethnic groups; and it can help to promote equality in society by providing positive images and role- models, encouraging individuals to realise their potential.

Forms of bias

In written form, including in words used in presentations, some people may well be able to evaluate the materials presented to them; others may believe in 'the authority of the printed word'. There is always a danger of presenting material as pure, objective 'facts'; where the assumption is that it is value-free. In fact, white culture and values are often presented as the norm, superior to all others; knowledge selected from a Eurocentric viewpoint is presented as all that is worth knowing and necessarily 'correct'.

There can also be a danger of being 'Anglo centric', ignoring Scotland, Wales and Northern Ireland; or of using 'American' when really referring to the United States.

This inherent bias of the text should be made explicit and as far as possible countered. The two most common forms of bias are omission and stereotyping.

Omission

All authors limit their discussion and exclude certain material. By including certain material, the author defines what is important. By excluding other points of view or experience, the author defines these as not important or valued. This can have tremendous influence on the reader's view of the subject. Only certain aspects of the world's art, music and beliefs are endorsed as being worthy of study; others are set against them as being less refined and certainly of less significance. Different forms of social organisation, economic development or scientific approach may similarly be disregarded or patronised as less significant than those in the so-called developed world.

A broader approach can thus improve the material for all readers but is particularly useful in making it relevant for minority ethnic readers. They are then able to identify with it, and to see their own heritage and culture being valued. A reader who cannot relate to the material, or who knows that it is at best partial or at worst misleading or incorrect, is unlikely to continue to engage with it.

Stereotyping

Stereotyping is the attribution of particular characteristics – appearance, temperament, potential etc.– to all members of an assumed group or 'race'. 'Race' is in fact a social and political construct rather than a biological one. Members of minority groups can sometimes be seen as deviant or threatening and subsequently stereotyped with negative characteristics – laziness or criminality for example. Even 'benign' stereotyping – as in the notions that all Asians are ambitious or that Muslim girls are passive – can be misleading and damaging.

Roles – social and occupational – are also often stereotyped and can become confounded with racist stereotypes. Black people, for example, are often portrayed in particular occupations, such as hospital cleaners and factory workers, which convey and confirm a status and position assigned to them by the majority culture. The choices made by many minority ethnic people to pursue higher status careers in law, medicine, and dentistry for example may also reinforce the viewpoint that different groups in society study different subjects. The reality is a far more complex picture and it is important to reflect this actual diversity and challenge the stereotype.

Checklist for multicultural material

• Avoid white supremacy thinking, for instance equating white with civilised or best, black with backward or of less worth.

• The diversity of contemporary British (or any other) society should be reflected: people of different ethnic groups and cultures should be portrayed, especially in case studies and illustrations. Ask yourself, is this the whole picture?

• Use examples which show people with a variety of attributes, whether of personal characteristics, lifestyles or occupational statuses.

• Don't make assumptions about people's national origin or religious or linguistic background.

• Make sure that cultures and societies are represented accurately, not from the point of view of the authors' ethnicity.

• Each culture has its own values and it is also by these that it should be evaluated; similarly, the diverse moral frameworks provided by different religions should be acknowledged where appropriate.

• Ask whether your text can be used by all people from a range of minority ethnic and religious backgrounds, in the

UK and internationally, particularly in the case studies and examples you have chosen.

Ethnicity

This is used to refer to the sense of identity which derives from membership of a group linked by different combinations of shared cultural characteristics, such as religion, language, history or geographical location. By this definition everyone belongs to an ethnic group, whether they are, in a given context, in the majority or in a minority. To stress this fact, when referring to a particular grouping of people, the phrase 'minority ethnic group' is recommended.

Black and Minority Ethnic

In the UK, 'Black people' generally refers either to people of African or Afro-Caribbean origin, including African-American or people born elsewhere with African or Afro- Caribbean heritage. Opinion is divided among British Asians on whether they consider themselves as black. However, this term probably does not cover adequately other groups such as those of Middle Eastern, North African or East Asian origin, or people of mixed origins. When a wider definition is needed, the term Black and Minority Ethnic (BME)' is widely used and accepted in the UK but may not mean much in other contexts. Therefore it is best to avoid generalisations of experience: it is better to state what groups are being discussed in a particular context.

'Black' with a capital 'B' is also used by some black people as a political term, this is to be considered when reading or interpreting communications.

Be sensitive to the use of phrases like 'blacken someone's character', 'working at the coal face', which equate 'black' with bad or complicated challenges and ideas.

Other terms

Avoid the terms 'non-white' and 'coloured' as these display white ethnocentrism – deviation from the supposed norm – which can obviously be offensive to black and minority ethnic people.

Use the term 'immigrant' appropriately: in the UK, it is often used incorrectly of people who are actually British nationals and have been born in the United Kingdom, or (again incorrectly) as a term which distinguishes black from white people. Many immigrants are white.

Use the term which different groups use about themselves: Inuit rather than Eskimo, Native American rather than Red Indian, or particular tribal names.

Ask for someone's first name or given name rather than their Christian name. Take the trouble to spell and pronounce people's names correctly.

You may find people, in particular Young People from East Asian countries such as Japan, China, South Korea and others use a 'Western Name'. If they offer you this it is their chosen name and should be respected.

Disability

The Disability Rights Commission estimates that around 10 million people in the UK are included in the definition of disability in the Disability Discrimination Act. Because of their 'invisibility' it is easy to forget that, for example, that not everyone:

- can leave their home at will

- has good eyesight and hearing

- is able to drive

- has the same amount of physical or mental energy as others.

This can lead to statements like; 'next time you walk into a shop' or 'when you are driving your car'. When talking about disabled people, it is easy to fall into traps arising from the viewpoint of a person without disabilities, which may exclude or offend members of your audience.

Marginalising

You will marginalise people who share a particular physical disability or have an identifiably different lifestyle by placing them in artificially homogeneous categories based on this one characteristic. Disabled people are especially vulnerable to this.

For instance, it is still relatively common practice to define people by their disability, using terminology such as 'epileptics'.

To talk instead of 'people with epilepsy' puts this characteristic into the perspective of a much wider life experience. 'People with disabilities' is a term which is commonly used but saying 'disabled people' is also acceptable as it emphasises that people are disabled by a society that doesn't accommodate them, rather than by their condition.

Patronising

All groups perceived as falling short of socially prescribed norms are likely to be seen as inferior in some way.

This might not be overt, but it's not always easy to avoid using patronising words, language or communications. Disabled people are especially vulnerable because the media and some charitable organisations reinforce an image of disabled people as 'unfortunate' and even 'pathetic' objects of patronage rather than as people with legitimate expectations and rights – to accessible public facilities, to employment, to a decent standard of living, for instance.

Condescending language such as 'Joe Bloggs is a polio victim' or 'confined to a wheelchair' should obviously be avoided. Equally undesirable is the portrayal of disabled people as courageous heroes, succeeding in some field despite their disability rather than because of their ability.

Blind people use terms like 'See you later' and can be irritated by well-meaning but clumsy attempts to avoid using 'see'. However, try not to use phrases that equate a physical condition with a shortcoming, like 'blind spot' or 'deaf to appeals'.

Use positive images of disabled people to illustrate your text, i.e. not as examples of disability but where the disability is incidental to the activity the person is doing. Try to avoid false or negative stereotypes: try to present an accurate representation of the variety of disabled people. For example, don't confine images to those of wheelchair users, who make up a very small percentage of people with disabilities.

Models of Disability

There are different ways of discussing disability. These are known as theoretical 'models' describing the thought process and understanding of disability. In countries with highly regarded records on human rights and disability they have learned that the Social model of disability is the only one which is fair and maintains the dignity of the Disabled Person. -Which is a UN convention recognised Human Right.

This brief article explores the different models of disability and suggests a minor addition. It's worth remembering, considering and mentioning in any training the immense about of human effort and activism taken by Disabled People to push for rights, in all counties, and to this day this important work is still being undertaken. Many, many lives of Disabled People have been cut short or abused due to organisations and governments not listening or working to the right model of disability. Disabled people of any background or race always have to work much harder to achieve any level of equality due to lack of social privilege, access to funding, unconscious bias or discrimination.

Charity Model of Disability

This model is a frequent failing of many organisations. A classic example where events, sponsorships, challenges, parties and alike are used to raise funds, highlight a cause or otherwise support a disabled person or community by people from outside whom no matter how well-meaning are acting in a way which disadvantages the Disabled Person though the requirement of gratitude and perception. The perception of Disabled people as 'Charity' or non-disabled people expecting thanks or gratitude for balancing their privilege.

Within this model is the concept of exercising privilege, you can 'pick and choose' which people or causes are worth of equipment you think they need. Re-enforcing or suggesting that they cannot make decisions, be a part of the conversation, make decisions, or undertake fundraising work for themselves.

Also in this category would be events or games which trivialise disability. Such as placing abled bodied people in wheelchairs or sighted people wearing blindfolds to experience an activity as a disabled person. No such activity gives you an insight into the lives of Disabled People and at worst makes it a loss of dignity. In this model too, we see some disabilities as something to 'fight' or 'challenge' rather than accepting without judgement.

Administrative Model of Disability

Here we have perhaps the second most dangerous model of inclusion. I say dangerous because applied in anyway this model actively discriminates and affects the health of Disabled People.

This is where systems and tests are developed to classify disabled people by their differences or inabilities. These classifications can then be used for a non-medical administration system to judge levels of benefits, services, equipment or access to support that person needs to live. -I use the word 'live' tenderly there as essentially an administration model is about keeping someone alive, not exploring or enhancing their quality of life, independence or dignity.

Medical Model of Disability

This is the most dangerous model of disability to work to. Sadly, it is one in the UK and elsewhere in Europe that comes up too often. It is primarily found in medical institutions, but also appears in Schools and local governance particularly those area with overlaps into the Specialised Needs in Education areas. It is worth noting that this is separate from a diagnosis or medical examinations for disabilities. Rather this is the thought model that leads beyond diagnosis into creating virtues of 'normal'.

Normal and definitions of normality are the critical factor in this model. Tests and procedures are used to classify and identify disabled people based on what medical practitioners think their disability is in relation to an idea of 'Normal'.

This can apply to identifying and killing Disabled People before they are born, imposing a pedestal of normality on a Disabled Person that cannot be achieved and actively discriminating against a person based on their medical classification.

Social Model of Disability

Equal rights. Dignity. Here we are at the only fair model of disability. One where society is seen as the disabling factor against a person, not the disability. This is the model which is protected and enshrined in law in the UK. Under this model society makes adjustments to include all people regardless of disability.

Access to goods and services are proceed from discrimination, health care and support are accessible and there is an enshrined dignity to the Disabled Person being the main voice in any discussions on their life or future.

It's worth noting that under this model Disabled People can contribute to society in a way which enhances culture, wealth and resilience. It allows for strength of community to develop and enhance the world in which we live by including more voices.

Economic Model of Disability

The last model of disability I discuss here is an extension perhaps of the social model, but one which I feel raises the points of inclusion. Here let's think of Disabled People as 'Another Customer'.

As discussed above the Social Model is from the concept of an individual focused problem to one of social context in that the disability is actually a function of the environmental and social constraints. A disability would not be a disability if the barriers of the society in which we live did not exist.

The social paradigm however relies on a social conscious or sense of social justice to implement the necessary structural changes to remove the barriers. -Not just complying with the minimum standards prescribed by law, but actually pro-actively removing these barriers.

In my view this is the crucial component missing from the Social Model dialogue.

The motivational factors for this to be implemented are still based on a human rights or fairness issue philosophy, one that has been enshrined in legislation and building laws to drive a social change forward.

The shortcomings of the social model is that the change has been driven as a rights issue and one of compliance that has been seen as a cost that society or organisations must pay for.

Here the social model laws can shift emphasis that it is all about access and not the person. The social model did shift the issue away from the individual to a broader context but did not actually change the focus or the attitudes into valuing a person with a disability as a valued and profitable customer or high value community member.

In other words, the legalities simply recognised that barriers are a broader social issue, but the social issue was still a problem to be solved.

Further the social model of disability by definition is prescriptive. It lays down a set of rules at a given point in time. Those rules define minimum requirements on both technical levels, for example ramp slopes, door widths, signage etc and in percentages for example the percentage of total cap spaces needed for people with a disability and the percentage of hotel rooms, picnic facilities etc.

It is driven by social expectations and translated by politicians and then implementors. At that point it ceases to be inclusive and just becomes another problem for organisations to deal with and is handed across to their many management departments.

The economic model is not one of risk mitigation or a reduction in law suit costs but rather one of valuing the economic input of a new customer or member. Business and organisations can ONLY gain from being more inclusive of all people, Disabled People especially will always have a higher regard for a brand or service that respects them and others.

In essence, be inclusive and work to the Social Model of Disability, but also acknowledge the Economic one as a way of increasing both the drive of society to change and also to perhaps make communities more prosperous for all by including Disabled People as customers or high value members of society.

Mental Health

Mental health is a state of well-being in which a person understands his or her own abilities, can cope with the normal stresses of life, can work productively and fruitfully, and is able to make a contribution to his or her community.

We all have a current state of Mental Health. Physical and mental health are the result of a complex interplay between many individual and environmental factors, including:

- family history of illness and disease/genetics

- lifestyle and health behaviours (e.g., isolation, smoking, exercise, substance use)

- levels of personal and workplace stress

- exposure to toxins & pollution

- Wealth and Socioeconomic status

- exposure to trauma (trauma can be any event outside of the individuals normal parameters of experience.)

- personal life circumstances and history

- access to supports (e.g., timely healthcare, social supports)

- individual's coping skills based on training and life experience.

When the demands placed on someone exceed their resources and coping abilities, their mental health will be negatively affected.

Mental illness

Mental illness is a recognised, medically diagnosable illness.

Which can result in the significant impairment of an individual's cognitive, affective or relational abilities.

Mental disorders result from biological, developmental and/or psychosocial factors and can be managed using approaches comparable to those applied to physical disease (i.e., prevention, diagnosis, treatment and rehabilitation).

In Language

It is important to remember we all at varying times have good and bad health and mental health. Therefore, it should always be discussed in the context as such.

Travellers

Travellers could be anywhere between 82,000 and 300,000 people within the UK. This includes the defined ethnic groups of Irish Travellers, Romany Gypsies and the undefined nomadic communities.

Romany Gypsies and Irish Travelers are defined as ethnic groups and protected from discrimination under the Equality Act 20104. With an estimated population of between two and twenty million Gypsies in Europe, they constitute the largest ethnic minority group on the continent.

There are a number of different groups who fall under the title of Gypsies and Travellers;

- Romany Gypsies

- Irish Travellers

- Scottish Gypsies and Travellers

- Welsh Gypsies and Travellers

- New Travellers

- Liveaboards, Bargees and others living in boats

- Travelling Showpeople

- Migrant workers

According to a recent government studies, Gypsies and Travellers are the least tolerated minority group in Northern Europe, with 58% of respondents in Britain reporting a negative impression of Gypsies, Roma and Travellers.

Much of the general public's opinion and knowledge on Gypsies and Travellers is reliant on news and media reports, entertainment coverage which can often be misinformed and reinforce many false stereotypes.

Inequalities faced by Gypsies and Travellers

Gypsies and Travellers, as well as experiencing discrimination can face challenges and difficulties in many aspects of life:

• Education - Of the people who identified as Gypsy or Traveller in the 2011 census of England and Wales, 60% had no formal qualifications whatsoever. This is three times higher than the national average.

• Health - Life expectancy of Gypsies and Travellers is ten years shorter than the national average.

• Prison - One in twenty prisoners identified as Gypsy, Roma or Traveller, despite the fact that only 0.1% of the population identify as Gypsy or Irish Traveller.

It is clear from these statistics that members of the Gypsy and Traveller community can face unique challenges and difficulties by virtue of their Traveller status, therefore some members may require extra help and assistance at times.

Nomadic lifestyle

An important element of Gypsy and Traveller culture is nomadism. Where possible, any arrangements which are compatible with a nomadic way of life should be considered when developing links with this community. This qualifies as a cultural.

As there is a severe shortage of places to pitch in the United Kingdom, some families may be living on unauthorised encampments.

Refugees

A refugee is a person who flees a nation or regime to escape persecution or violence.

An asylum seeker is an individual, unable or unwilling to return to her nation of origin, who seeks the protection of another nation.

To seek asylum in most countries an individual must have a well-founded fear of persecution based on their race, ethnicity, religion, or political or social associations.

Although the difference between these two groups rests on a technicality of international immigration law, they share the experience of being uprooted from their homes by tragic or violent circumstance.

The earliest international agreements on the treatment and protection of refugees date back to the plight of Jewish Holocaust victims after World War II. Allied-administered camps in Germany, Austria, Poland, and Italy housed over a quarter-million displaced persons (DPs). After its founding, the United Nations also administered aid and provided housing to DPs, but a long-term solution was slow in its evolution. Many victims did not have family or homes to which they could return; others feared further persecution or simply did not wish to return.

In 2002, there were approximately sixteen million refugees across the globe who fled conflict and warfare.

In 2019 that number is estimated at around 33.5 Million and growing. This brief introduction to immigration has chosen to focus on refugees in a trans-national context—those who have fled across international borders seeking refuge. The millions of internally displaced persons who have fled strife, but remained within their national borders, these are not reflected in any UN figures.

Refugees, Migrants and Asylum seekers are all protected under UN Human Rights Agreements. As such, including when being discussed in writing, film, speech or online they have the same rights to dignity, respect, freedom and privacy as non-refugees. They should never be discussed in a criminalised way.

It is important to note the disproportion of Black Refugees highlighting the fact that effects such as climate change are leading to emerging race related pressures not affecting the more privileged white communities.

Diverse groups

Refugees can be of any race, any sexual orientation, may or may not be disabled, be young or old, and will have a gender and a sex. It is important to never assume or stereotype.

Refugees with more resources may have access to mobile phones, laptops or computers. This does not mean they have any wealth, but simply have a recognition of the value of keeping safe via technology.

We are at a stage where the number of transient humans on the planet is growing. This will have to be factored into any Equalities, Diversity and Inclusion planning in the future.

Gender & Sex

English language still tends to assume the world to be male unless proved otherwise. This sees 'male' as the standard, with 'female' a deviation from the norm.

This tendency to exclude half of society is increasingly being challenged and being sensitive to the ways in which we use gender-specific words can promote more positive attitudes to equality. Confronting sexism means not just avoiding discriminatory expressions but thinking about positive ways to include women, men and emerging gender terms on equal terms.

Family & Gender roles

A decreasing minority of households take the form of the idealised 2+2 family. Reflect this reality in illustrations as well as what you write. Show women in jobs, hobbies, roles and situations traditionally ascribed to men and vice versa. It is important to realise a 'Family' can be of one parent and one child through to no parents and many children. Families can also include LGBT+ Couples in various parental roles or simply be a couple. It is also Show people of varying physical appearance, and Disabled People and not just 'idealised' fictional types.

Language

The words we use can reflect the different standards applied to women and men. Avoid irrelevant modifiers like 'woman doctor' or 'male nurse'; the stereotypes implied by terms such as 'working mother' or 'housewife'; and the feminine (i.e. non-standard and often belittling) forms of nouns: actress, comedienne, usherette, hostess, poetess, manageress, and heroine.

The same words may have different connotations when used of women and men: 'ambitious', for instance, could denote approval of a man, but is often disparaging when said of a woman. Conversely, 'manly' qualities are often complimentary when ascribed to a woman, whereas 'feminine' qualities are usually meant to be derogatory if applied to men. Women are trivialised by the use of different words to describe their actions: men talk but women gossip. The test is always: would what I have said about this person mean the same and sound right if I said it of someone of the other sex?

In the same way, it is still common for women to be unnecessarily referred to in terms of their appearance, their marital status, their role rather than their actions, and by their first name or social title. Again, always ask yourself whether you would describe or address a man in the same way. 'Girl' is patronising to an adult woman, and so often is 'lady': use them only where it would be appropriate to refer to males as 'boys' or 'gentlemen'.

'Man'

'Man' at one time meant only 'person' or 'human being'. Although it technically still has this generic meaning, 'adult male person' tends to be the image the word calls up. Using 'man' in the generic sense can make it easy to slip from generalisations about people into generalisations about men only. This can be misleading or confusing. Don't, however, fall into the trap of using a generic gender-neutral term but then subconsciously assigning male gender to it, for example; 'We shared a table with two Koreans and their wives'.

She or He?

An unconscious bias occurs when using the term 'he' to refer to any unspecified person, An attempt to justify this either on the grounds that anything else is grammatically incorrect or on the grounds that that 'everyone knows' that 'he' includes 'she', cannot be defended.

The blanket use of 'he' makes it unclear just who is being included. 'He or she' (and there's no reason for the 'he' to come first) is clumsy if it has to be repeated often, but 's/he', 'you' and 'one' are available.

The subject could be made plural, or your sentence could be written so as to avoid the need for a pronoun. A disclaimer that 'he' should be taken to include 'she' looks like the token gesture it is.

There are circumstances when gender-specific terms accurately reflect reality, for example in historical texts. But in most cases it is preferable to use gender-neutral terms. Think about what you actually mean, and who you are really referring to. It may be better to recast your sentence rather than to substitute one word for another.

Sexual Orientation

There is generally much more awareness about the lives of lesbian, gay and bisexual people than there was twenty years ago.

This is in part the result of the many, many campaigners, activists and people willing to speak out to discuss equality for LGBT+ people in the last century. It is also the result of new civil and legal protections and arising from this an increased openness by gay, lesbian and bisexual people. Created by the people mentioned above.

In the past, imagery of gay and lesbian people was generally confined to narrow stereotypes; the effeminate entertainer, the male hairdresser and the 'butch' lesbian for example.

Today, gay people can be open about their sexuality while serving in the armed forces, have an equal age of consent to sexual activity, the right to adopt and foster children and the right to form a civil partnership or marry (In most of the UK) giving the same rights and responsibilities as heterosexual married couples.

There is a greater recognition that gay people are immersed in all aspects of society, all kinds of occupations and are part of families and local communities.

Despite these changes, there are still many people who don't accept lesbian and gay sexuality. There is still much ignorance, prejudice and fear in some people's attitudes this community. Sometimes the press is responsible for helping to sustain this intolerance, forming and reinforcing attitudes that provoke harassment, discrimination and hostility.

Homophobic and Transphobic bullying, harassment and discrimination, in schools is still considered by LGBT+ organisations to be a widespread problem.

Accurate, positive, diverse and informed images of LGBT+ people should be presented in our University material. As equal members of society in words they should be described in terms that do not trivialise or demean them, do not encourage discrimination or distorted images of their lives, do not sensationalise their activities, or imply any form of illegality or immorality.

Where the experiences of lesbian, gay and bisexual people are different, then inclusion of particular experience in course and other materials, highlights our understanding

240

and acceptance of the worth and value of different lives. Don't introduce issues of sexual orientation gratuitously, but where it is relevant, include it in a fair and objective way.

Language Guidelines

The term 'homosexual' is generally not used now, as it has medical origins and derogatory connotations, and is often taken to refer only to men.

Avoid 'heterosexism' (for example, phrases like 'the natural attraction between the sexes'). Don't suddenly switch from 'we' to 'they' in discussing issues around sexual orientation.

Avoid negative stereotyping of supposed characteristics of lesbians, bi-sexual, trans and gay men. Don't perpetuate myths such as that 'gay people' are less suited to be parents, or are incapable of steady relationships, or are emotionally unstable.

Use 'partner' instead of 'spouse', and don't assume that everyone belongs to a traditional fictional family image.

Avoid implying any form of sympathy, that LGBT+ people or their families and friends are less fortunate, unhappy, or present a 'problem'.

Never suggest that lesbian, trans, bi or gay sexual orientation is 'abnormal', 'perverted', 'immoral', or an illness. It is factually incorrect.

If discussing colleagues or people it is important not to stereotype or assume. It is inappropriate to ask a person's sexual orientation.

Coming Out

The process through which a person acknowledges and accepts their sexual orientation or gender identity and shares this with others.

This is not something which non-LGBT+ people have experience in or a similar life history. It is important to not belittle, switch to comedy or dismiss a person whom is discussing their coming out.

Homeless

Homelessness is a growing issue, not just in the UK but across the world. Young People, Older People, Ex-Service Personnel and Disabled People are the communities being most affected by this emerging issue.

In communities across the country, people are increasingly aware of the sight of people who are without a home, sleeping in parks, sitting on pavements or asking for money.

There is developing an institutional 'So-What' attitude to this across the entire population as an attempt to dismiss the challenge presented when faced with a person whom is homeless.

As with all areas of the community it is vitally important to present homeless people in a positive, dignified and considered way. Use the term Homeless Person as a term over any other negative slang.

Unconscious Bias

A 'Bias' is a prejudice in favour of or against one thing, person, or group compared with another usually in a way that's considered to be unfair. Biases may be held by an individual, group, or institution and can have negative or positive consequences. An example would be a lean towards Homophobia, Racism or other types of discrimination, this isn't a direct discrimination statement, merely an internal judgement that is misinformed by such a bias.

There are two main types of biases:

- Conscious bias (also known as explicit bias)

- Unconscious bias (also known as implicit bias)

It is important to note that biases, conscious or unconscious, are not limited to ethnicity and race. Though racial bias and discrimination are well documented, biases may exist toward any social group.

One's age, gender, gender identity physical abilities, religion, sexual orientation, weight, and many other characteristics are subject to bias.

Unconscious biases are social stereotypes about certain groups of people that individuals form outside their own conscious awareness. Everyone holds unconscious beliefs about various social and identity groups, and these biases stem from one's tendency to organize social worlds by categorizing.

Unconscious bias is far more prevalent than conscious prejudice and often incompatible with one's conscious values. Certain scenarios can activate unconscious attitudes and beliefs. For example, biases may be more prevalent when multi-tasking or working under time pressure. In circumstances where an individual or organisation has been impacted negatively, be that legal, media or internal complaints. These over times can create the idea of an 'issue' or 'problem' with a certain community or characteristic. Even if this against the individual or organisation's ethos and ethics.

Individual strategies to address unconscious bias include:

- Promoting self-awareness: recognising one's biases using third party training is the first step.

- Understanding the nature of bias is also essential. The strategy of categorization that gives rise to unconscious bias is a normal aspect of human cognition. Understanding this important concept can help individuals approach their own biases in a more informed and open way.

- Opportunities to have discussions, with others (especially those from socially dissimilar groups) can also be helpful. Sharing your biases can help others feel more secure about exploring their own biases. It's important to have these conversations in a safe space-individuals must be open to alternative perspectives and viewpoints.

- Facilitated discussions and training sessions promoting bias literacy utilising the concepts and techniques listed about have been proven effective in minimising bias.

- Accepting that EVERYONE will have a form of unconscious bias.

- Institutional Strategies

Recommended for good practice, all institutions and organisations should:

- Develop concrete, objective indicators & outcomes for hiring, evaluation, and promotion to reduce standard stereotypes. This is recognising and self-checking in-house bias.

- Develop standardised criteria to assess the impact of individual contributions in performance evaluations.

- Develop and utilise structured interviews and develop objective evaluation criteria for staff training and development.

- Provide unconscious bias training workshops for all staff and core workers / volunteers.

Privilege

Across the world, people of all backgrounds are experiencing a time in which discussions about race, gender, gender identity, sexual orientation, religion, and culture are often at the forefront of their everyday lives.

A great many people avoid these discussions because they fear that conversations about race, bias, and racism lead to feelings of anger, guilt, discomfort, sadness, and at times disrespect.

However now is the time when we need to be discussing these key human rights movements to ensure we not only overcome, but we also create a fairer world for all.

While uncomfortable for some, the thought might be, the young people of the world are perhaps best placed to facilitate the dialogue to bring about positive, productive outcomes. -Put simply, they can make friends with less unconscious and conscious bias.

This brief introduction is intended to engage in constructive dialogue about privilege, prejudice, power, and the ways that all of us can work together to shift the conversation from hate and violence toward understanding and respect to ultimately bring about positive change and unity to our communities.

In our global society, each of us has an identity that shapes how we see ourselves and others. Not only do our social norms and cultural underpinnings influence our experiences, they also set the course for how we view the world. Differences in identity—and related struggles for place and power—are woven throughout our history and social and political culture.

While diversity is always a strength, and one historically proven, the path toward common ground, mutual respect, dignity, and equality has been a long and often bloodstained struggle for nearly every faith, race, sex, disability, sexuality and ethnic group.

The world's most difficult challenges are not creation of peace or stopping wars but getting to the causes of conflict such as such as poverty, disenfranchisement, isolation, inequity, and violence.

You may have guessed by now, but there is no solving of these situations without discussing the role of privilege.

While Male Privilege is perhaps the widest form example of this, here we are going to start to discuss race. This is because race is a strong factor in privilege and perhaps the most uncomfortable for a white person to discuss. Again, myself as a White Male person from a reasonably developed country which has laws protecting inclusion, have to acknowledge that even in writing and choosing the topic, is an exercise in privilege, but one I hope is fully acknowledged by myself.

The Role of Privilege

For many members of the western-majority culture (i.e., those who identify as White), being made aware of one's classification as linked to privilege is likely not a common or welcomed experience.

Indeed, many people have never been asked or required to reflect on their own privileged status, and in regard to racial identity, doing so might feel uncomfortable or even argue with the common narrative regarding social and political changes over the years.

For example, White people may attach the concepts of progress toward equality or being "colour blind" as mitigating privilege. As a result, many White people either may not be aware of or may avoid considering how simply being White confers special status or experiences, potentially to the detriment of others.

While many White Westerners may not view themselves as privileged because of their economic or social status, the advantage of being in the majority racial group is real, even if often hidden.

Consider simple life activities such as shopping in a store without the fear of being followed by a security guard or buying or renting a home in an area that you can afford without consideration of your race.

This fundamental disconnect might both motivate and exacerbate the racial/cultural divides, due to a lack of awareness of how privilege contributes to the realities of racism. We are all taught 'Racism is bad!' but are we taught about how our privileges may be equally bad?

Importantly, although privilege is often associated only with wealth and/or economic status, it applies far more broadly. Privilege can be assigned to populations within a group, such as athletes, individuals perceived as attractive, individuals who attain higher levels of education, or membership in certain faith/no-faith groups. Loosely defined, privilege includes the following aspects.

Unearned advantages that are highly valued but restricted to certain groups by birth or status.

Unearned advantages are those that someone receives by identifying or being born into a specific group. It is important to note that the groups who have received these advantages have not earned them due to their own hard work but rather their affiliation (e.g., being born into a wealthy family provides privileges that others do not have, such as accessing education as well as mental health and medical services; White People in the west are more likely to walk into a store without the suspicion of stealing).

Equally important to note is the reality that while some benefit from unearned advantages, others are victims of unearned disadvantage. Unearned entitlements are things of value that all people should have; however, they are often restricted to certain groups because of the values of the majority culture that influence political and social decisions.

"Members of the privileged group gain many benefits by their affiliation with the dominant side of the power system. Privileged advantage in societal relationships benefits the holder of privilege, who may receive deference, special knowledge, or a higher comfort level to guide societal interaction.

Privilege is not visible to its holder; it is merely there, a part of the world, a way of life, simply the way things are. Others have a lack, an absence, a deficiency."

Privilege exists when one group has something of value that is denied to others simply because of group membership and not based on what a person or group has done or failed to do.

For those who routinely benefit from privilege, the challenge is to not quickly deny its existence. It is important to recognise that privilege is a part of the reality that helps some while it impedes others' experiences.

For example, although being female or a person of colour does not necessarily directly determine an outcome, these characteristics can easily and quickly make these individuals less likely to be hired, recognized, or rewarded in a variety of situations.

Privilege is problematic when it skews our personal interactions and judgments and also when it contributes to blinding us to societies' barriers for those who do not possess a certain privilege, thereby creating or perpetuating inequity.

In Western culture, certain groups have the privilege of operating within settings—through no effort on their part—that are more conducive for their success, while others—through no fault of their own—find themselves in settings that make success more difficult.

Again, this concept refers to any advantage that is unearned, exclusive, and socially conferred. For example, with White privilege, White people are generally assumed to be law abiding until they show that they are not. Even then a lighter crime or wrong-doing is often assigned by any form of justice.

On the other hand, Muslims, Black People, and other races are routinely assumed to be criminals or potential criminals until they show that they are not.

"the lives we lead affect what we are able to see and hear in the world around us."

WILDMAN & DAVIS (1995)

Recognising your privileges.

An important first step to understanding the concept of group-based privilege and how it can shape peoples' perspectives, experiences, and interactions is to examine our own experience.

We can be the beneficiary of privilege without recognizing or consciously perpetuating it. Learning to see one's own privilege as well as that of groups and systems can create an important pathway to self-discovery. Some questions to consider are listed below.

- When was the last time you had to think about your ethnicity, race, gender identity, ability level, religion, and/or sexual orientation? What provoked you to think about it or acknowledge it?

- When watching TV or a movie, how likely are you to watch shows whose characters reflect your ethnicity, race, gender, ability level, religion, gender identity, and/or sexual orientation?

- When using social media, how diverse is your feed? How diverse are your friends and followers? How diverse are those that you follow?

- How do you respond when others make negative statements towards individuals of a different ethnicity, race, gender, ability level, religion, sexual orientation, and/or gender identity than yourself?

- How often do you go to social settings where the majority of individuals are of a different ethnicity, race, gender, ability level, religion, sexual orientation, and/or gender identity than yourself?

- How diverse is the community in which you live?

- How do you feel when you are in a community that is different than your neighbourhood?

- How would you make your neighbourhood more inclusive and sensitive?

- If you recognised your privilege, what will you now do with this realisation?

Suggestions for Talking to Others About Privilege

Engaging in thoughtful discussion with people of other backgrounds is essential to understanding privilege.

Start by discussing how privilege looks in our society and which groups have privilege, and which do not.

The first discussion should be about privilege, in general, and the reasons some groups have privilege and others do not. This lays a foundation before personalising the discussion and may help participants be less defensive.

Next, ask participants to discuss examples of how they are privileged and how they are not privileged. Listen to the ways in which a person legitimately does and does not have privilege and validate any frustrations that are expressed, especially before offering your opinion or perspective. The discussion about areas in which participants have not experienced privilege is where the most empathy may be found.

Be sure to listen twice as much as you speak.

Always recognise and respond to your own privileges in any discussions. Stress that privilege is relative to each individual's lived experience.

The degree to which individuals experience privilege must be framed within the context of their own race, gender, ability level, religion, sexual orientation, and/or gender identity coupled with the communities in which they live, work, and play as well as the persons with whom they interact.

Recognise that having privilege does not require feeling guilty for your privilege.

Because each of us likely has an element of privilege within our make-up (ethnicity, gender, ability level, religion, sexual orientation, and/or gender identity), individuals need not feel guilty for their privilege.

Rather, the focus should be to use our privileged positions to challenge the systems in which we live. Specifically, challenge yourself and others to refuse to live in a system of unchecked privilege.

For example, challenging school staff members to walk the route their students take to school each day is a small but meaningful step toward helping them to identify and understand their privilege in relation to the students.

Determine and offer ways to challenge systems of privilege and oppression in your own life.

If someone mentions an oppressive pattern that relates to privilege (e.g., "Men always dominate conversations and talk over women because they are taught that their voices are more valuable."), consider how you will not participate in this pattern. For example, you might say less or be aware of how often you are speaking and begin to listen more while others are speaking.

Learn and use

Understanding and engaging in self-reflection and discussions about privilege is an essential step to addressing individual and institutional in-equality and discrimination in our society.

We must be aware of and honest about our personal perspectives and how these may or may not contribute to biases that in turn may contribute, even unintentionally supporting; prejudice, inequity, isolation, poverty, and perhaps violence.

Accessibility for type, print and information design

Definition of Print Disability

A print-disabled person is anyone for whom a printed piece of information is unable to fully or easily access that information. This can be compounded by visual, cognitive, or physical disability. You do not need to a Disabled Person to be affected by Print Disability, rather it is the material itself which is the disabling factor.

Format of materials

Consider in mind the needs of all people in the physical design of your information. You could consider making it available in Braille or large print, or as an audiotape; and you could add subtitles to your video.

Physical attributes

Glossy paper and coloured print on a coloured background make reading difficult for anyone.

Colour-blindness is a common issue that will often create enhanced barriers when presented with an unconsidered piece of information design.

Think too about ease of physical handling: could a heavy book be split up, or if a ring binder, which is easier to open, would be a more appropriate format.

There are no legally defined minimum standards for clear print and large print. However good practice for Inclusive Design and Accessibility would mean:

Presentation & Printing

- Document has not been created by enlarging with a photocopier (other than exceptional cases)

- A4 paper used unless content or purpose dictates otherwise

- No information conveyed solely through colour, images or diagrams

- No text overlapping images (other than exceptional cases) Paper is non-glossy

- Paper is of sufficient weight to avoid show-through

- Identification and navigation of document

- Layout is clear and consistent

- Headings are clearly differentiated from text

- Appropriate use of page numbers

Typefaces

- Minimum text size of 12 point for clear print, ideally 14 point

- Minimum text size of 16 point for large print, ideally minimum of 18 point

- Text such as page numbers, labels, superscripts is ideally the same size as the body text

- Legible sans-serif typeface such as Arial or Helvetica.

- No italics, underlining or large blocks of capital letters

- Adequate line spacing

- Adequate space between paragraphs

- Text is left aligned (un-justified) except in exceptional circumstances

- All text is horizontal

- Good contrast between text and background

Accuracy in large print, audio and braille adaptions

- Document is an accurate representation of the original un-adapted document and tested.

- Quality control measures in place (e.g., proofing, testing production equipment, regular servicing etc)

Finishing and packaging

- Appropriately bound Appropriately packaged

- Clearly labelled

- Cover is non-glossy

- Requests are despatched in good time

- Adapted versions are despatched in no more time than the non-adapted version.

Accessibility for websites and onscreen media.

The Internet is intended to be designed to work for all people, whatever their hardware, software, language, location, or ability.

When information on the internet meets this criteria it is accessible to people with a diverse range of hearing, movement, sight, and cognitive ability.

The internet and other onscreen media should be empowering, removing barriers to communication and interaction that many people face in the physical world.

However, when web sites, applications, technologies, or tools are badly designed, they can create barriers that exclude people from using this new modern pinnacle of communication.

The internet and other onscreen media must be accessible to provide equal access and equal opportunity to people with diverse abilities. Indeed, the UN Convention on the

Rights of Persons with Disabilities recognises access to information and communications technologies, including "the Web", as a basic human right.

Screen and Internet Accessibility

It is recommended to visit the W3C website for full details on making your website compliant and inclusive for all. However addressed here are some of the basic criteria for inclusion and accessibility for websites and on screen media:

- Alternative Text for Images - Images should include equivalent alternative text (alt text) in the markup/code.

- Keyboard Input – Options for keyboard input allow for people whom cannot use a mouse, including many users with limited fine motor control. An accessible website does not rely on the mouse; it makes all functionality available from a keyboard.

- Assistive technologies that mimic the keyboard, such as speech input can be tagged and allowed for very easily on any website.

- Transcripts for Audio available for read-a-loud software.

Further information:

Web Accessibility Initiative (WAI) at W3C
The W3C Web Accessibility Initiative (WAI) brings together people from industry, disability organizations, government, and research labs from around the world to develop guidelines and resources to help make the Web accessible to people with auditory, cognitive, neurological, physical, speech, and visual disabilities.

Key International Human Rights Agreements

Below is a list of current international agreements relating to Equality, Diversity, Inclusion and Human Rights. This list is intended to be a reference point for note only.

United Nations & other global Declarations

Declaration of the Rights of the Child 1923

Universal Declaration of Human Rights (UN, 1948)

Declaration on the Rights of Disabled Persons (UN, 1975)

Declaration on the Right to Development (UN, 1986)

Vienna Declaration and Programme of Action (World Conference on Human Rights, 1993)

Declaration of Human Duties and Responsibilities (UNESCO, 1998)

Universal Declaration on Cultural Diversity (UNESCO, 2001)

Declaration on the Rights of Indigenous Peoples (UN, 2007)

UN declaration on sexual orientation and gender identity (UN, 2008)

United Nations Conventions

Convention on the Elimination of All Forms of Racial Discrimination (ICERD, 21 December, 1965)

International Covenant on Civil and Political Rights (ICCPR, 16 December, 1966)

International Covenant on Economic, Social, and Cultural Rights (ICESCR, 16 December, 1966)

Convention on the Elimination of All Forms of Discrimination Against Women (CEDAW, 18 December, 1979)

Convention against Torture and Other Cruel, Inhuman or Degrading Treatment or Punishment (CAT, 10 December, 1984)

Convention on the Rights of the Child (CRC, 20 November, 1989)

International Convention on the Protection of the Rights of All Migrant Workers and Members of Their Families

(ICMW, 18 December, 1990)

International Convention for the Protection of All Persons from Enforced Disappearance (CPED, 20 December, 2006)

Convention on the Rights of Persons with Disabilities (CRPD, 13 December, 2006)

Additional agreements covering Human Rights

International Convention on the Suppression and

Punishment of the Crime of Apartheid (ICSPCA)

Convention Relating to the Status of Refugees and Protocol Relating to the Status of Refugees

Convention on the Reduction of Statelessness

Convention on the Prevention and Punishment of the Crime of Genocide

Indigenous and Tribal Peoples Convention, 1989 (ILO 169)

European Agreements and Conventions

Charter of Fundamental Rights of the European Union

Convention on Action against Trafficking in Human Beings

European Convention on Nationality

European Charter for Regional or Minority Languages (ECRML)

European Convention on Human Rights (ECHR)

European Convention for the Prevention of Torture and Inhuman or Degrading Treatment or Punishment (CPT)

European Social Charter (ESC), and Revised Social Charter

Framework Convention for the Protection of National Minorities (FCNM)

UK Equality, Diversity and Inclusion Legislation

The Human Rights Act 1998 sets out the fundamental rights and freedoms that everyone in the UK is entitled to. It incorporates the rights set out in the European Convention on Human Rights (ECHR) into domestic British law. The Human Rights Act came into force in the UK in October 2000.

The Equality Act 2010 came into force from October 2010 providing a modern, single legal framework with clear law to better tackle disadvantage and discrimination.

Gender Recognition Act to make provision for and in connection with change of gender. There are current changes that may be brought into force at a future date.

Updates to this guide & new emerging terms

I very much consider this book as version 1. It is a base to be used, engaged with and built upon.

If I have a fact incorrect or am missing a key piece about your community I apologise and welcome the corrections and your support in making this resource more inclusive.

It is also important to realise that society evolves and moves on. As I have said previously, this book is never intended to be read cover to cover, but rather referenced as a guide. If a term you need is missing, if a community is not listed. Please help me add this to the next edition.

For all changes and suggestions please email me at: studio@tonymalone.co.uk

About the author

Tony Malone, an artist, a Buddhist Master and a Global Human Rights Advisor. He is also a volunteer in the World Scouting Movement for Diversity & Inclusion.

Tony has over 20 years' experience quietly being at the forefront of many areas of human and environmental rights campaigning and consultancy.

He frequently lectures at universities and colleges across the world and is a much sought-after Inclusion speaker for governments and corporations.

Currently working on projects which support the rights, safety and dignity of youth refugees.

Find out more at: **tonymalone.co.uk**

Also by Tony Malone:

The essential quick reference guide to Human Rights in the United Kingdom. Intended for Activists, Students and anyone with an interest in Human Rights.